Curriculum Development 2005

Curriculum Development 2005

Towards Learning without Burdern and
Quality of Education – An Evaluation

J.C. Aggarwal

S. Gupta

SHIPRA

Rs. 495, US$ 13

ISBN: 978-81-7541-263-7

2026 Impression, PoD
(2nd Enlarged & Rev. Ed. 2007,
First Published 2005)

Curriculum Development 2005

Published by:
SHIPRA PUBLICATIONS
LG 18-19, Pankaj Central Market
I.P. Ext., Patparganj, Delhi 110092, India
91 11 47322068; 9650028065, 9810522367
info@shiprapublication.com
www.shiprapublication.com

"When I was a child I had the freedom to make my own toys out of trifles and create my own games from imagination. In my happiness my playmates had their full share; in fact the complete enjoyment of my games depended upon their taking part in them. One day, in this paradise of our childhood, entered a temptation from the market world of the adult. A toy bought from an English shop was given to one of our companions; it was perfect, bit and wonderfully life-like. He became proud of the toy and less mindful of the game; he kept that expensive thing carefully away from us, glorying in his exclusive possession of it, feeling himself superior to his playmates whose toys were cheap. I am sure if he could have used the modern language of history he would have said that he was more civilised than ourselves to the extent of his owning that ridiculously perfect toy.

One thing he failed to realise in his excitement – a fact which at the moment seemed to him insignificant – that this temptation obscured something a great deal more perfect than his toy. the revelation of the perfect child. The toy merely expressed his wealth, but not the child's creative spirit, not the child's generous joy in his play, his open invitation to all who were his compeers to his play-world".

*From **Civilisation and Progress** by Rabindranath Tagore*

Preface to the Revised Edition

The author is grateful to the readers for their positive response to this publication.

Following Chapters are added in the revised edition:

- Major Observations and Recommendations of National Curriculum Framework—NCF (2005).
- Curriculum Construction and Central Board of Secondary Education.
- Curriculum and Textbooks.

J.C. Aggarwal

Preface to the First Edition

In 1992, the Human Resource Development Ministry appointed the National Advisory Committee under the Chairmanship of Prof. Yash Pal, former Chairman University Grants Commission to advise on the ways and means to reduce the load on school students at all levels. The Committee submitted it report, entitled '*Learning without Burden*'. Shri Arjun Singh was the then Minister of Human Resource Development. In 2004, the same Ministry under the charge of the same Minister appointed the same distinguished philosopher-scientist, the Chairman of the Steering Committee on Curriculum which according to the Ministry was to be formulated in the light of the findings of the '*Learning without Burden*' (1993) It may be recalled that the findings, observations and recommendations of the Committee were reviewed by a Group in 1993, on the Reduction of Academic Burden on School Education. The Group commented upon each recommendation and made further observations also and the matter ended there. Since 1993, both the reports have been gathering dust in the archives. One fondly hopes the history won't repeat itself as regards the implementation of National Curriculum Framework (NCF).

Earlier in 1985, the NCERT set up an in-house Working Group to make a quick appraisal of the curriculum load at the school level. The report *inter alia arrived at the following conclusions.*

1. The failure to provide the pre-requisites for the effective

transaction of curriculum to the problem of curriculum load.

2. The problem of curriculum load is more a problem of educational management and resource constraints than a problem of curriculum development.

There has been no appreciable change in the present scenario.

In this context, the observations of the learned chairman (Prof. Yash Pal), of the report '*Learning without Burden*' (1993) deserve special mention and due consideration. "On a personal note I would like to add that this has been a difficult report to write. Not because we had a great deal of trouble understanding the problem, or that we had a lot of differences among ourselves, or even developing a conviction that something was to be done the difficulty for me personally has come from my inability to persuade myself that the 'state' of our school education is an independent variable—that it could be altered without altering lot of things in our social set-up! Indeed, it is not only the set-up in the country but also the defective interpretation of the external scenario, that finally impacts our young students, robbing them a wholesome growth and depriving the country of what they could contribute."

One may raise the question–has there been any change in the situation?

It is our considered view that not, withstanding platitudes of the report, its tryout in some schools must be taken up for a year so. In case it is rewarding, the recommendations must be operationalised across the country's schools.

Since repeated references are made in the Draft National Curriculum Framework (NCF) 2005, to the Report '*Learning without Burden*', for reading reference of the readers, its recommendations along with the comments of the Group are given in the appendix.

The Constitution and functions of the Central Advisory Board as reconstituted in July 2004 are given in Appendix 2. It may be recalled that CABE is the highest advisory body to advise the Central and State Governments in the field of education. The National Curriculum Framework (NCF) was placed before it for its approval in July 2005.

There has been a good deal of talk on providing quality education. In this regard, the main recommendations of the UNESCO International Conference on Education (September 2004) on the theme 'Quality Education for All Young People: Challenges, Trends and Priorities' are given in Appendix 3. We acknowledge with thanks NCERT for quoting the draft of National Curriculum Framework 2005 and its Website preceding to our observations on it, in this book. It is hoped that these observations/comments may lead to further debate on this issue of national importance among the different sections engaged in the field of education.

Contents

1

Foreword, Executive Summary and Members—Curriculum 2005

In the preliminary pages of the draft of National Curriculum Framework 2005, Shri Yash Pal, Chairperson, writes in his *Foreword*:

"I have had the privilege of participating in a remarkable process of social deliberation initiated by NCERT to focus public attention on what should be taught to our children and how. In the course of this wideranging churning of ideas and expectations, I have worked closely with a large number of very special individuals for the preparation of the National Curriculum Framework presented in this document. The names of these individuals are given in this document.

There is much analysis and lot of advice. All this is accompanied by frequent reminders that specificities matter, that mother tongue is a critical conduit, that social, economic and ethnic backgrounds are important for enabling children to construct their own knowledge. Media and educational technologies are recognised as significant, but the teacher remains central. Diversities are emphasised but never viewed as problems. There is a continuing recognition that societal learning is an asset and formal curriculum will be greatly enriched by integrating with that. There is a celebration of plurality and an understanding that within a broad framework plural approaches would lead to enhanced creativity.

The document frequently revolves around the question of curriculum load on children. In this regard we seem to have fallen into a pit. We have bartered away understanding for memory—based short term information accumulation. This must be reversed, particularly now that the mass of what could be memorised has begun to explode. We need to give our children some taste of understanding, following which they would be able to learn and create their own versions of knowledge as they go out to meet the world of bits, images and transactions of life. Such a taste would make the present of our children wholesome, creative and enjoyable;

they would not be traumatised by excessive burden of information that is required merely for a short time before the hurdle race we call examination. The document suggests some ways of getting out of this self-imposed adversity. Achieving some degree of success in this area would also signify that we have learnt to appreciate the capacity for learning and the futility of filling up children's memory banks with information that is best kept as ink marks on paper or bits on a computer disc.

Education is not a physical thing that can be delivered through post or a teacher. Fertile and robust education is always created, rooted on physical and cultural soil of the child and nourished through interaction with parents, teachers, fellow students and community. The role and dignity of teachers in this function must be strengthened and underlined. There is mutuality to genuine construction of knowledge. In this transaction the teacher also learns if the child is not forced to remain passive. Since children usually perceive and observe more than grownups, their potential role as knowledge creators needs to be appreciated. From personal experience I can say with assurance that a lot of my limited understanding is due to my interaction with children. The document does dwell on this aspect.

The richness and comprehensive nature of this document would not have been achieved without a special ignition that enveloped all those who got involved. I do not know who struck the spark—perhaps no one in particular. Perhaps the effort happened at a point in time when a critical mass of discomfort had accumulated. Enough is enough, was the feeling amongst most of the participants. Perhaps the enthusiasm of a few was infectious.

It was tempting to assign blame for many things that have not gone as well as we wished many decades ago. We have tended to avoid the blame game—perhaps due to the fact that we are all responsible in some way or another. Most of us are responsible, as members of a middle class that had begun to emotionally secede from the mass of people in the country. I was struck by the frequency of words like 'pluralism', 'equity' and 'equality'. I do not believe they are part of a political rhetoric, because we talked very little politics in our extensive discussions. I believe this came about because we were led to a conviction that our strength lies in the presently deprived three fourth of our people. Marrying their socially acquired competences and skills with academic pursuits in our educational institutions would lead to a special flowering.

The document suggests ways of moving in that direction. Some of the systemic changes suggested would definitely help. We do not feel daunted by the task. We feel it is doable. I hope this effort might start a freedom movement for education of our young—away from some of the tyrannies in which we have enveloped ourselves."

OBSERVATION ON THE FOREWORD

After going through the inspiring and thought-provocating foreword of the Chairperson of the National Steering Committee, and specially of the concluding remarks: "I hope this effort might start a freedom movement for education of our young—away from some of the tyrannies in which we have enveloped ourselves" one is reminded of the following titles:

1. De-Schooling Society by Ivan Illich
2. The School is Dead by Everett Reimer.
3. Compulsory Miseducation by Paul Goodman.
4. Pedagogy of the Oppressed by Paulo Freire.
5. How Children Fail by John Holt
6. How Children Learn by John Holt
7. The Underachieving School by John Holt
8. Look at Kids by Leila Berg
9. Counter Course by Trevor Pateman
10. Teaching a Subversive Activity by Charles Weingratner and Neil Postman
11. Essays on Education by Jules Henry
12. 36 children by Herbert Kohl
13. The Lives of Children by George Dennism
14. Cultural Action for Freedom by Paulo Freire
15. Celebration of Awareness by Ivan Illich D.
16. My Pedagogic Creed by John Dewey
17. Schools of Tommorrow by John Dewey

The following titles written by Indian authors may also be placed in this category.

1. My School by Rabindranath Tagore.
2. A Poet's School by Rabindranath Tagore
3. Education and the Significance of Life by J. Krishnamurti.
4. Problems of Educational Reconstruction by K.G. Saiyiadain
5. Curriculum Load at the School Level: A Quick Appraisal by NCERT.
6. Learning Without Burden by Yash Pal Committee Report
7. Report by the Group on the Reduction of Academic Burden on School Education, M.H.R.O. (Chaturvedi Report.
A VERY LAUDABLE I DEAL

Executive Summary

The Executive Committee of NCERT had taken the decision, at its meetings held on 14 and 19 July 2004, to revise the National Curriculum Framework, following the statement made by the Hon'ble Minister of Human Resource Development in the Lok Sabha that the Council should take up such a revision. Subsequently. Education Secretary. Ministry of HRD communicated to the Director of NCERT the need to review the National Curriculum Framework for School Education (NCFSE-2000) in the light of the report. *Learning without Burden* (1993). In the context of these decisions, a National Steering Committee, chaired by Prof Yash Pal and 21 National Focus Groups were set up. Membership of these committees covered institutions of advanced learning, NCERTs own faculty, school teachers and non-government organizations. Consultations were held in all parts of the country, in addition to five major regional seminars held at the NCERTs Regional Institutes of Education in Mysore. Ajmer, Bhopal, Bhubaneswar and Shillong. Consultations with State Secretaries. NCERTs. and examination boards were carried out. A national conference of rural teachers was organized to seek their advice. Advertisements were issued in national and regional newspapers to invite public opinion and a large number of responses were received.

The revised National Curriculum Framework (NCF) opens with a quotation from Rabindranath Tagore's essay *Civilisation and Progress,* in which the poet reminds us that "creative spirit" and 'generous joy' are key in childhood, both of which can be distorted by an unthinking adult world. The opening chapter discusses curricular reform efforts made since independence. The National Policy on Education-(NPE. 1986) proposed National Curriculum Framework as a means to evolve a national system of education, recommending a core component derived from the Vision of national development enshrined in the Constitution. The Programme of Action (POA, 1992) elaborated this focus by emphasizing relevance, flexibility and quality.

Seeking guidance from the Constitutional vision of India as a secular, egalitarian and pluralistic society, founded on the values of social justice and equality, certain broad aims of education have been identified in this document. These include independence of thought and action, sensitivity to others' well being and feelings, learning to respond to new situations in a flexible and creative manner, pre-disposition towards participation in democratic processes, and the ability to work towards and contribute to economic processes and social change. For teaching to serve as a means to strengthen our democratic way of life. it must respond to the presence of first generation school goers, whose retention is imperative owing to the Constitutional amendment which has made elementary education a fundamental right of every child. Ensuring health, nutrition and an inclusive school environment support ail children in their learning irrespective of caste, gender, disability, is enjoined upon us by the Constitutional amendment.

The fact that learning has become a source of burden and stress on children is an evidence of a deep distortion in educational aims and quality. To correct this distortion, the present NCF proposes four guiding principles for curriculum development:

(i) connecting knowledge to life outside the school: (ii) ensuring that learning shifts away from rote methods: (iii) enriching the curriculum so that it goes beyond textbooks: and (iv) making examinations more flexible and integrating them with classroom life.

All our pedagogic efforts during the primary classes greatly depend on professional planning and significant expansion of Early Childhood Care and Education (ECCE). Indeed, the revision of primary school syllabi and textbooks needs to be undertaken in the light of the well known principles of ECCE. The nature of knowledge-and children's own strategies of learning are discussed in Chapter 2 which formulates a theoretical basis for the recommendations made in Chapter 3 in the different curricular areas. The fact that knowledge is constructed by the child implies that curriculum, syllabi and textbooks should enable the teacher to organize classroom experiences in consonance with the child's nature and environment, and providing opportunities for all children. Teaching should aim at enhancing children's natural desire and strategies to learn. Knowledge needs to be distinguished from information, and leaching needs to be seen as a professional activity, not as coaching for memorization or as transmission of facts. Activity is the heart of the child's attempt to make sense of the world therefore every resource must be deployed to enable children to express, handle objects, explore their natural and social milieu, and to grow up healthy. If children's classroom experiences are to be organized in a manner that permits the child to construct knowledge, then our school system requires substantial systemic reforms (Chapter 5) and reconceptualization of curricular areas or school subjects (Chapter 3) and resources to improve the quality of the school ethos (Chapter 4)

In all the four familiar areas of school curriculum, i.e. language, mathematics, science and social sciences, significant changes are recommended with a view to making education more relevant to the present day and future needs and in order to alleviate the stress children are coping with today. This NCF recommends the softening of subject boundaries so that children can get a taste of integrated knowledge and joy of understanding. In addition, plurality of textbooks and other material, which could incorporate local knowledge and traditional skills, and a stimulating school environment which responds to the child's home and community environment, are also suggested. In language, a renewed attempt to implement the three language formula is suggested. alongwith an emphasis on recognition of children's mother tongues, including tribal languages, as the best medium of instruction. The multilingual character of Indian society should be seen as a resource to promote multilingual proficiency in every child, which includes proficiency in English. This is possible only if learning builds oh a sound language pedagogy in the mother tongue. Reading and writing, listening and speech contribute to the child's progress in all curricular areas and must be the basis for curriculum planning. Emphasis on reading throughout the primary classes is necessary to give every child a solid foundation for school learning.

The teaching of mathematics should enhance the child's resources to think and reason, visualize and handle abstractions, to formulate and solve problems. This broad spectrum of aims can be covered by teaching relevant and important mathematic, embedded in the child's experience. Succeeding in mathematics should be seen as the right of every child. For this widening in its scope and relating it to other subjects is essential. The infrastructural challenge involved in making computer hardware, software, and connectivity to every school should be pursued.

The teaching of science should be recast so that it enables children to examine and analyse everyday experiences. Concern for the environment should be emphasized in every subject and through a wide range of activities, involving outdoor project work. A social movement along the lines of *Children's Science Congress* should be visualized in order to promote discovery learning across the nation, and eventually throughout South Asia.

In social sciences, the approach proposed in the NCF recognizes disciplinary markers while emphasizing integration on significant themes, such as water. A paradigm shift is recommended, proposing the study of social sciences from the perspective of marginalized groups. Gender justice and sensitivity towards tribal and dalit issues and minority sensibilities must inform all sectors of the social science. Civics should be recast as political science, and the significance of history as a shaping influence on the child's conception of the past and civic identity should be recognized.

This NCF draws attention to four other curricular areas: work, the arts and heritage crafts, health and physical education. and peace. In the context of work, certain radical steps to link learning from the primary stage upwards with work arc suggested on the ground that work transforms knowledge into experience and generates important personal and social values, such as self-reliance, creativity and cooperation. It also inspires new forms of knowledge and creativity. At the senior level, a strategy to formally recognize out-of-school resources for work is recommended, to benefit children who opt for livelihood-related education. Such out-of-school agencies need accredition so that they can provide 'work benches' where children can work with tools and other resources. Craft mapping is recommended to identify zones where vocational training in craft forms, involving local craft persons, can be made available to children.

Art as a subject at all stages is recommended, covering all four major spheres, i.e. music, dance, visual arts and theatre. Emphasis should be on interactive approaches. not instruction, because the goal of art education is to promote aesthetic and personal awareness and the ability to express oneself in different forms. The importance of India's heritage crafts, both in terms of their economic and aesthetic values, should be recognized as being relevant to school education.

The child's success at school depends on nutrition and a well-planned physical activity programmes, hence resources and school time must be deployed for the strengthening of the mid-day meal programme. Special efforts are needed to ensure that girls receive as much attention in health and physical education programmes from the pre-school stage upwards as boys.

Peace as a pro-condition for national development and as a social temper is proposed as a comprehensive value-framework which has immense relevance today, in view of the growing tendency across the world towards intolerance and violence as a way to resolve conflicts. The potential of peace education for socializing children into a democratic and just culture can be actualized through appropriate activities and judicious choice of topics in all subjects and at all stages. Peace education as an area of study is recommended for inclusion in the curriculum for teacher education.

The school ethos is discussed as a dimension of curriculum, as it predisposes the child towards the aims of education and strategies of learning necessary for success at school. As a resource, school time needs to be planned in a flexible manner. Locally planned, flexible school calendars and time tables which permit time slots of different lengths required for different kinds of activities, such as project work and outdoor excursions to natural and heritage sites, are recommended. Efforts are required to prepare more learning resources for children, especially books and reference materials in regional languages, for school and teacher reference libraries, and access to interactive rather than disseminative technologies. The NCF emphasizes the importance of multiplicity and fluidity of options at the senior secondary level, discouraging the entrenched tendency to place children in fixed streams, and limiting opportunity of children especially from the rural areas.

In the context of systemic reforms, this document emphasises strengthening the Panchayati Raj Institutions by the adoption of a more streamlined approach lo encourage community participation as a means of enhancing of quality and accountability. Academic planning and leadership at the school level is essential lo improve quality, strategic differentiation of roles is necessary at block and cluster-levels. In teacher education, radical steps are required to reverse the recent trend towards the dilution of the professional norms recommended by the Chattopadhyaya Commission (1984). Pro-service training programmes need to be more comprehensive and lengthy, incorporating sufficient opportunities for observation of children and integration of pedagogic theory with practice through school internship.

Examination reforms constitute the most important systemic measure to be taken for curricular renewal and to find a remedy for the growing problem of psychological pressure that children and their parents feel, especially in Classes X and XII. Specific measures include changing the typology of the question paper so that reasoning and creative abilities replace memorization as the basis of evaluation, and integration of examinations with classroom life by encouraging transparency and internal assessment. The stress on pro-board examinations must be reversed and strategies to enable children lo opt for different levels of attainment should be encouraged to overcome the present system of generalized classification into 'pass' and 'fail' categories.

Finally, the document recommends partnerships between the school system and other civil society groups, including non-governmental organizations, and teacher organizations. The innovative experiences already available should be mainstreamed. and awareness of the challenges implied in the Universalization of Elementary Education (UEE) should become a subject of wide ranging cooperation between the state and all agencies concerned about children.

Observations on Executive Summary

The Executive Summary begins with the statement that the decision to revise the National Curriculum Framework was taken following the statement of the Hon'ble Minisetr of Human Resource Development in the Lok Sabha. It is silent on the contents of the statement. It, therefore, passes one's comprehension as to the terms of the reference of the Steering Committee.

The next statement refers to the communication of the Education Secretary, Ministry of HRD to the NCERT to review the National Curriculum Framework for School Education (NCFSE-2000) in the light of the Report of the '*Learning without Burden*' (1993). In this context it is observed that the said Report was examined by a Group on the Reduction of Academic Burden on School Education (1993-94), constituted by the MHRD. Y.N. Chaturvedi, Additional Secretary, Department of Education, MHRD was the chairperson of the group. The Group gave parawise recommendations and also made additional observations. What happened thereafter is not known.

For ready reference both the reports are given in Appendix 1.

Members of the National Steering Committee

1. Prof. Yash Pal (*Chairperson*), Former Chairman University Grants Commission 11B, Super Deluxe Flats Sector 15A, NOIDA Uttar Pradesh

2. Acharya Ramamurti Chairman Sharam Bharti, Khadigram, P.O. Khadigram Dist. Jamui – 811 313 Bihar

3. Dr. Shailesh A. Shirali Principal Amber Valley Residential School K.M. Road. Mughihalli Chikmagalur – 577 101 Karnataka

4. Shri Rohit Dhankar Director, Digantar, Todi Ramzanipura Khonagorian Road, P.O. Jagatpura Jaipur – 302 025 Rajasthan

5. Shri Poromesh Acharya (Former Member Education Commission, West Bengal)

6. Dr. Mina Swaminathan Hony. Director Uttara Devi Centre for Gender and Development M.S. Swaminathan Research Foundation, 3rd Cross Road Taramani Institutional Area Chennai – 600 113 Tamil Nadu

7. Dr. Padma M. Sarangapani Associate Fellow National Institute of Advanced Studies Indian Institute of Science Campus Bangalore – 560 012 Karnataka

8. Prof. R. Ramanujam Institute of Mathematical Science 4th Cross, CIT Campus Tharamani, Chennai-600 113 Tamil Nadu

9. Prof. Anil Sadgopal (Department of Education, Delhi University) E-8/29A, Sahkar Nagar Bhopal – 162 039 Madhya Pradesh

10. Prof. G. Ravindra Principal, Regional Institute of Education (NCERT) Manasgangotri, Mysore – 570 006 Karnataka

11. Prof. Dr. (Ms.) Damyanti J. Modi
(Former Head, Education Department
Bhavnagar University)
2009, A/2, Ananddhara
Near Vadodaria Park. Hill Drive
Bhavnagar – 364 002, Gujarat

12. Ms. Sunila Masih
Teacher, Mitra G.H.S. School
Sohagpur, P.O.
Dist. Hoshangabad – 461 771
Madhya Pradesh

13. Ms. Harsh Kumari
Headmistress, CIE,
Experimental Basic School
Department of Education
University of Delhi
Delhi – 110 007

14. Shri Trilochan Dass Garg
Principal, Kendriya Vidyalaya
Faridkot Cantt. Pubjab

15. Prof. Arvind Kumar
Centre Director
Homi Bhabha Centre for Science Education, V.N. Purao Marg.
Mankhurd, Mumbai – 400 088
Maharashtra

16. Prof. Gopal Guru
Centre for Political Studies
School of Social Science
Jawaharlal Nehru University
New Delhi – 110 067

17. Dr. Ramachandra Guha
22 A, Brunton Road
Bangalore – 560 025, Karnataka

18. Dr. B.A. Dabla
Professor & Head
Department of Sociology & Social Work. University of Kashmir
Srinagar – 190 006
Jammu & Kashmir

19. Shri Ashok Vajpeyi
(Former Vice-Chancellor
Mahatma Gandhi International Hindi University)
C-60, Anupam Apartment
B-13, Vasundhara Enclave
Delhi – 110 096

20. Prof. Valson Thampu
St, Stephens Hospital
G-3, Administration Block
Tis Hazari Delhi – 110 054

21. Prof. Shanta Sinha
Director, M. Venkatarangaiya Foundation
2001, Narayan Apartments
West Marredpally
Secunderabad – 500 026
Andhra Pradesh

22. Dr. (Mrs) Vijaya Mulay
(Founder Principal, CET, NCERT)
President, India Documentary Producers Association
B-42, Friends Colony (West)
New Delhi – 110 065

23. Prof. Mrinal Miri
Vice Chancellor
North Eastern Hill University
P.O. NEHU Campus
Mawkynroh Umshing
Shillong – 793 022,
Meghalaya

24. Prof. (Mrs.) Talat Aziz
IASE, Faculty of Education
Jamia Milia Islamia
Jamia Nagar,
New Delhi – 110 025

25. Professor Savita Sinha
Head, DESSH. NCERT
Sri Aurobindo marg
New Delhi – 110 016

26. Professor K.K. Vassishtha
Head, DEE, NCERT
Sri Aurobindo Marg
New Delhi – 110 016

27. Dr. Sandhya Pranjpe
DEE, NCERT
Sri Aurobindo marg
New Delhi – 110 016

28. Professor C.S. Nagaraju
Head, DERPP. NCERT
Sri Aurobindo Marg
New Delhi – 110 016

29. Dr. Jyotsna Tiwari
DESSH. NCERT
Sri Aurobindo Marg
New Delhi – 110 016

30. Professor M. Chandra
Head DESM, NCERT
Sri Aurobindo Marg
New Dehi – 110 016

31. Dr. Anita Julka
Reader, DEGSN, NCERT
Sri Aurobindo Marg
New Delhi – 110 016

32. Prof. Krishna Kumar
Director, NCERT
Sri Aurobindo Marg
New Delhi – 110 016

33. Mrs. Ania Kaul
Secretary, NCERT
Sri Aurobindo Marg
New Delhi – 110 016

34. Shri Ashok Ganguly
Chairman, Central Board of Secondary Education
Shiksha Kendra
2, Community Centre
Preet Vihar,
Delhi – 110 092

35. Prof. M.A. Khader (*Member Secretary*)
Head, Curriculum Group
NCERT, Sri Aurobindo Marg
New Delhi – 110 016

OBSERVATIONS

A perusal of the Composition of the Steering Committee reveals that no representative of a government school finds place on the Committee. Likewise it has no representative of a public school. Out of 35 members, fifteen are drawn from the Colleges of Education/NCERT. Three, including the chairman were on the Committee that submitted the report '*Learning without Burden*'. Thus the composition of the Committee is unbalanced. It would have been better to include practising teachers on the Committee to provide more meaningful and pragmatic approach.

Source: Draft National Curriculum Framwork 2005, NCERT and its website.

2

Perspective

The chapter 1 of the draft is on Perspective and states as under:

1.1 INTRODUCTION

India is a free nation with a rich variegated history, an extraordinarily complex cultural diversity and a commitment to democratic values and well-being for all. Ever since 1986 when the National Policy on Education was approved by Parliament, efforts to redesign the curriculum have been focused on the creation of a national system of education. Given the enormity and importance of the task of educating the country's children, it is necessary that from time to time, we create occasions to collectively sit back and ask ourselves, "What is it that we are doing in our engagement with this task? Is it time for us to refresh what we provide to our children in the name of education?"

If we look at what the system of education has accomplished since Independence, perhaps we have much to be satisfied with. Today, our country engages nearly 55 lakh teachers spread over around 10 lakh schools to educate about 2025 lakh children. While 82 per cent of habitations have a primary school within a radius of one kilometre, there is an upper primary school within 3 kilometers for 75 per cent of habitations. At least 50 per cent of our children who appear at the school leaving examinations passout of the secondary school system. Despite these trends, 37 per cent people of India lack literacy skills, about 53 per cent children drop out at elementary stage and over 75 per cent of our rural schools are multigrade. Further, there is a deep disquiet about several aspects of our educational practice: (a) the school system is characterised by an inflexibility which makes it resistant to change; (b) learning has become an isolated activity which does not encourage children to link knowledge with their lives in any organic or vital way; (c) schools promote a regime of thought which discourages creative thinking and insights; (d) what is presented and transmitted in the name of learning in schools bypasses vital dimensions of the human capacity to create new knowledge; (e) the "future" of the child has taken centre-stage to the near exclusion of the child's "present", which is detrimental to the well-being of the child as well as the society and the nation.

The basic concerns of education—to enable children to make sense of life and develop their potential, to define and pursue a purpose and recognise the right of others to do the same—stand uncontested and valid even today. If anything, we need to reiterate the mutual interdependence of humans, and as Tagore says, we achieve our greatest happiness when we realise ourselves through others. Equally, we need to reaffirm our commitment to the concept of equality, within the landscape of cultural and socio-economic diversity from which children enter into the portals of the school. Individual aspirations in a competitive economy tend to reduce education to becoming an instrument of material success. The perception, which places the individual in exclusively competitive relationships, puts unreasonable stress on children, and thus distorts values. It also makes learning from each other a matter of little consequence. Education must be able to promote values which foster peace, humaneness and tolerance in a multi-cultural society.

This document seeks to provide a framework within which teachers and schools can choose and plan experiences that they think children should have. In order to realise educational objectives, the curriculum be conceptualised as a structure which articulates required experiences. For this it should address some basic questions:

(a) What educational purposes should the schools seek to achieve?
(b) What educational experiences can be provided that are likely to achieve these purposes?
(c) How can these educational experiences be meaningfully organised?
(d) How do we ensure that these educational purposes are indeed being accomplished?

The review of National Curriculum Framework, 2000 was initiated specifically to address the problem of curriculum load on children. A committee appointed by the Ministry of Human Resource Development in the early 1990s had analysed this problem, tracing its roots to the system's tendency to treat information as knowledge. In its report, *Learning without Burden,* the Committee pointed out that learning at school cannot become a joyful experience unless we change our perception of the child as a receiver of knowledge and move beyond the convention to use textbooks as the basis for examination. The impulse to teach everything arises from lack of faith in children's own creative instinct and the capacity to construct knowledge out of their experience. The size of textbooks has been growing over the years, even as the pressure to include new topics mounts and the effort to synthesize knowledge and treat it holistically gets weaker. Flabby textbooks and the syllabi they cover symbolise a systemic failure to address children in a child-centred manner. Those who write such encyclopaedic textbooks are guided by the popular belief that there has been an explosion of knowledge. Therefore, vast amounts of knowledge should be pushed down little children's throats in order to catch up with other countries. *Learning without Burden* recommended a major change in the design of syllabi and textbooks, and also a change in the social ethos, which places stress on children to become aggressively competitive and exhibit precocity. To make teaching a means of harnessing the child's creative nature, the report recommended a fundamental change in the matter of organising the school curriculum, and also in the system of examination which forces children to memorise information and to reproduce it. Learning for the sake of being examined in a mechanical manner takes away the joy of being young and delinks school knowledge from everyday experience. To address this deep structural problem the present document draws upon and elaborates on the insights of *Learning without Burden.*

Rather than prescribe, this document seeks to enable teachers and administrators and other agencies involved in the design of syllabi and textbooks and examination reform make rational choices and decisions. It will also enable them to develop and implement innovative, locale specific programmes. By contextualising the challenges involved in curriculum renewal in contemporary social reality, this document draws attention to certain specific problems which demand an imaginative response. We expect that it will strengthen ongoing processes of reform, such as devolution of decision making to teachers and elected local level bodies, while it also identifies new areas for attention such as the need for plurality of textbooks and urgent improvement in the examination system.

1.2 RETROSPECT

Mahatma Gandhi had visualised education as a means of awakening the nation's conscience to injustice, violence and inequality entrenched in the social order. *Nai Talim* emphasised self-reliance and dignity of the individual which would form the basis of social relations characterised by non-violence within and across society. Gandhiji recommended the use of the immediate environment, including the mother tongue and work, as a resource for socialising the child into a transformative vision of society. He dreamt of an India in which every individual discovers and realises her or his talents and potential by working with others towards restructuring the world, which continues to be characterised by conflicts between nations, within society and between humanity and nature.

After independence, the concerns of education articulated during the freedom struggle were revisited by the National Commissions – the Secondary Education Commission (1952-53) and Education Commission (1964-66). Both Commissions elaborated on the themes emerging out of Mahatama Gandhi's educational philosophy in the changed socio-political context with a focus on national development.

Education under the Indian Constitution till 1976 allowed the State Governments to take decisions on all matters pertaining to school education, including curriculum, within their jurisdiction. The Centre could only provide guidance to the States on policy issues. It is such circumstances, that the initial attempts of the National Education Policy of 1968 and the Curriculum Framework designed by NCERT, in 1975 were formulated. In 1976 the constitution was amended to include education in the Concurrent List and for the first time in 1986 the country as a whole had a uniform National Policy on Education. The NPE (1986) recommended a common core component in the school curriculum throughout the country. The policy also entrusted NCERT with the responsibility of developing National Curriculum Framework and review the framework at frequent intervals.

NCERT in continuation of its curriculum related work carried out studies and consultation subsequent to 1975 and had drafted a curriculum framework as a part of its activity in 1984. This exercise aimed at making school education comparable across the country in qualitative terms and also make it a means to ensure national integration without compromising on the country's pluralistic character. Based on such experience the Council's work culminated in the National Curriculum Framework for School Education, 1988. However, the articulation of this framework through courses of studies and textbooks in a rapidly changing developmental context resulted in an increase in 'curricular load' and made learning at school a source of stress for young minds and bodies during their formative years of childhood and adolescence. This aspect has been coherently brought out in the report of the Committee under the chairmanship of Professor. Yash Pal entitled *Learning Without Burden, 1993.*

1.3 NATIONAL CURRICULUM FRAMEWORK

In spite of the recommendations of the NPE-1986 to identify competencies and values to be nurtured at different stages, school education came to be driven more and more by high stake examinations based on information loaded textbooks. Despite the review of the Curriculum Framework in 2000, the vexed issues of curriculum load and the tyranny of examinations remained unresolved. The current review exercise takes into recognisance both positive and negative developments in the field and attempts to address the future requirements of school education at the turn of the century. In this endeavour several inter-related dimensions are kept in mind namely, the aims of education, the social milieu of children, the nature of knowledge in its broader sense, the nature of human development and the process of human learning.

The term National Curriculum Framework is often wrongly construed to mean that an instrument of uniformity is being proposed. The intention as articulated in the NPE, 1986 and the Programme of Action (PoA) 1992 was quite the contrary. NPE proposed a national framework for curriculum as a means to evolve a national system of education capable of responding to India's diversity of geographical and cultural milieus while ensuring a common core of values along with academic components. "The NPE-PoA envisaged a child centred approach to promote universal enrolment and universal retention of children upto 14 years of age and substantial improvement in the quality of education in the school." (PoA page 77). The PoA further elaborated on this vision of NPE by emphasising relevance, flexibility and quality as characteristics of the national curriculum framework. Thus both these documents envisioned the National Curriculum Framework as a means to modernise the system of education.

1.4 GUIDING PRINCIPLES

We need to plan and pay attention to systemic matters that will enable us to implement many of the good ideas that have already been articulated in the past. Paramount among these are:

- connecting knowledge to life outside the school,
- ensuring that learning is shifted away from rote methods,
- enriching the curriculum to provide for overall development of children rather than remain textbook centric, and
- making examinations more flexible and integrated with classroom life.

In the present context there are new developments and concerns to which our curriculum must respond. The foremost among these is the importance of including and retaining all children in school, through a programme which reaffirms the value of each child and enables all children to experience dignity and the confidence to learn. Curriculum design must reflect the commitment to Universal Elementary Education (UEE), not only in representing cultural diversity, but also by ensuring that children from different social and economic backgrounds with variation in physical, psychological and intellectual characteristics are able to learn and achieve success in school. In this context, disadvantages in education arising from inequalities of gender, caste, language, culture, religion or disabilities need to be addressed directly, not only through policies and schemes but also through the design and selection of learning tasks and pedagogic practices, right from the period of early childhood.

UEE makes us aware of the need to broaden the scope of curriculum to include in it the rich inheritance of different traditions of knowledge, work and crafts. Some of these traditions today face a serious threat from market forces and commodification of knowledge in the context of the globalisation of the economy. The development of self-esteem and ethics and the need to cultivate children's creativity must receive primacy. In the context of a fast changing and competitive global context, it's imperative that we respect children's native wisdom and imagination.

Decentralisation and emphasis on the role of Panchayati Raj Institutions are major steps towards systemic reforms taken in the recent past in education. These steps also entail the responsibility to localise knowledge and curriculum practices. PRIs offer an opportunity to make the system less bureaucratic, and the school more autonomous.

Making children sensitive to environment and its protection is another important curricular concern. The emergence of new technological choices and living styles witnessed during the last century has led to environmental degradation and vast imbalances between the advantaged and the disadvantaged. It has become imperative now more than ever before to nurture and preserve the environment. Education can provide the necessary perspective on how human life can be reconciled with the crisis of the environment so that survival, growth and development remain possible. The National Policy on Education 1986 emphasised the need to create awareness of environmental concerns by integrating it in the educational process at all stages of education and for all sections of society.

Living in harmony within oneself and with one's natural and social environment is a basic human need. Sound development of an individual's personality can take place only in an ethos marked by peace. A disturbed natural and psycho-social environment often leads to stress in human relations, triggering intolerance and conflict. We live in an age of unprecedented violence—local, national, regional and global. Education often plays a passive, or even insidious, role allowing young minds to be indoctrinated into a culture of intolerance, which denies the fundamental importance of human sentiments and the noble truths discovered by different civilisations. Building a culture of peace is an incontestable goal of education. Education to be meaningful should empower individuals to choose peace as a way of life and enable them to become managers rather than passive spectators of conflict. Peace as an integrative perspective for school curriculum has a potential to become an enterprise for healing and revitalising the nation.

As a nation we have been able to sustain a robust democratic polity. The vision of democracy articulated by the Secondary Education Commission (1952) is worth recalling:

> "*Citizenship in a democracy involves many intellectual, social and moral qualities...a democratic citizen should have the understanding and the intellectual integrity to sift truth from falsehood, facts from propaganda and to reject the dangerous appeal of fanaticism and prejudice ... should neither reject the old because it is old nor accept the new because it is new, but dispassionately examine both and courageously reject what arrests the forces of justice and progress....*". For us to foster democracy as a way of life rather than only a system of governance, the values enshrined in the constitution assume paramount significance.

- The Constitution of India guarantees equality of status and opportunity to all citizens. Continued exclusion of vast numbers of children from education and the disparities caused through private and public school systems challenge the efforts towards equality. Education should function as an instrument of social transformation and an egalitarian social order.
- Justice—social, economic and political—to all citizens is integral to strengthening democracy.
- Liberty of thought and action is a fundamental value embedded in our constitution. Democracy requires as well as creates a kind of citizen who pursues her own autonomously chosen ends and respects others' right to do so.
- A citizen needs to internalize the principles of equality, justice and liberty to promote fraternity among all.
- India is a secular democratic state, that means that all faiths are respected, but at the same time the Indian state has no preference for any particular faith. The felt need, today, is to inculcate among children a respect for all people regardless of their religious beliefs.

India is a multicultural society made up of numerous regional and local cultures. People's religious beliefs, ways of life and their understanding of social relationships are quite distinct from one another.

All the groups have equal rights to co-exist and flourish, and the education system needs to respond to the cultural pluralism inherent in our society. To strengthen our cultural heritage and national identify, the curriculum should enable the younger generation to reinterpret and re-evaluate the past with reference to new priorities and emerging outlooks of a changing societal context. Creation of a citizenry conscious of their rights and commitment to the principles embodied in our constitution is a prerequisite in this context.

1.5 THE QUALITY DIMENSION

Even as the system attempts to reach every child, the issue of quality presents a new range of challenges. The belief that quality goes with privilege is clearly irreconcilable with the vision of participatory democracy India upholds and practises in the political sphere. Its practice in the sphere of education demands that the education available to all children in different regions and sections of society has a comparable quality. The late J.P. Naik had described equality, quality and quantity as the 'elusive triangle' of Indian education. Dealing with this metaphorical triangle requires deeper theoretical understanding of quality than has been available. UNESCO's recently published global monitoring report discusses systemic standards as the appropriate context of the quality debate. From this point of view, the child's performance needs to be treated as an indicator of systemic quality. In a system of education which is divided between a fast growing private sector and a larger state sector marked by shortage and uneven spread of resources, the issue of quality poses complex conceptual and practical questions. The belief that private schools have higher quality treats examination results as the sole criterion for judging quality. This kind of perception ignores the ethos-related limitations of the privileged private schools. The fact that they often neglect the child's mother tongues warrants us to wonder about the opportunities they are able to provide to the child to construct knowledge in meaningful ways. Moreover, the exclusion of the poor from their admission process implies the loss of learning opportunities which occur in a classroom with children from diverse socioeconomic and cultural backgrounds.

Physical resources by themselves cannot be regarded as an indicator of quality; yet, the extreme and chronic shortage of physical resources, including basic infrastructural amenities, in schools run by the state or local bodies does present a serious quality constraint. The availability of qualified and motivated teachers who perceive teaching as a career option applies to all sectors of schools as a necessary pre-condition for quality. Recent suggestions for the dilutions of standards in teacher recruitment, training and service conditions articulated in the NPE and, before it, by the Chattopadhyaya Commission (1984) arouse anxiety. No system of education can rise above the quality of its teachers, and the quality of teachers greatly depends on the means deployed for selection, procedures used for training, and the strategies adopted for ensuring accountability.

The quality dimension also needs to be examined from the point of view of the experiences designed for the child in terms of knowledge and skills. Assumptions about the nature of knowledge and the child's own nature shape the school ethos and the approaches used by those who prepare the syllabi and textbooks, and by teachers. The representation of knowledge in textbooks and other materials need to be viewed from the larger perspective of the challenges facing humanity and the nation today. No subject in the school curriculum can stay aloof from these larger concerns, and therefore, the selection of knowledge proposed to be included in each subject area requires careful examination in terms of socio-economic and cultural conditions and goals. The greatest national challenge for education is to strengthen our participatory democracy and the values enshrined in the Constitution. Meeting this challenge implies that we make quality and social justice the central theme of curricular reform. Citizenship training has been an important aspect of formal education. Today, it needs to be boldly reconceptualised in terms of the discourses of universal human rights and the approaches associated with critical pedagogy. A clear orientation towards values associated with peace and harmonious co-existence is called for. Quality in education includes a concern for quality of life in all its dimensions. This is why a concern for peace, protection of the environment and a predisposition towards social change must be viewed as a core component of quality, not merely as value premises.

1.6 THE SOCIAL CONTEXT OF EDUCATION

The education system does not function in isolation from the society of which it is a part. Hierarchies of caste, economic status and gender relations, cultural diversity as well as uneven development that characterize Indian society, also deeply influence access to education and participation of children in schools. This is reflected in the sharp disparities between different social and economic groups which are seen in school enrolment and completion rates. Thus, girls belonging to dalit and adivasi communities among the rural and urban poor are educationally most vulnerable. In urban locations and many villages, the school system itself is stratified and provides children with strikingly different educational experiences.

Schools range from the high cost 'public' (private) schools, to which the urban elite send their children, to the ostensibly 'free' poorly functioning local body run primary schools where children from hitherto educationally deprived communities predominate. A striking recent feature is the growth of multigrade schools in rural areas, based on mechanical application of 'teacher pupil ratios' to the need to provide a school within 1km of each habitation, yet unsupported by necessary curricular concepts or clarity on materials or pedagogy. Such developments unintentionally reinforce privilege and exclusion in education and undermine the constitutional value of equality of opportunity and social justice. If 'free' education is understood as 'removal of constraints' to education, then we must realize the importance of other sectors of the state's social policy for supporting and facilitating the achievement of UEE.

Globalisation and the spread of market relations in every sphere of society have important implications for education. On the one hand, we are witnessing the increasing commercialisation of education, and on the other, inadequate public funding for education and the official thrust towards 'alternative' schools indicate a shifting of responsibility for education from the state to families and communities. We need to be vigilant about the pressures to commodity schools and the application of market related concepts to schools and school quality. The increasing competitive environment into which schools are being drawn and the aspirations of parents places a tremendous burden of stress and anxiety on all children, including the very young, to the detriment of their personal growth and development and inculcating in them the joy of learning.

The 73rd and 74th constitutional amendments and the institutionalised statutory space they provide for local communities to participate in decision making in education for their children are important developments. However, parental aspirations for education are belied by endemic poverty and unequal social relations, and by lack of adequate provision of schooling of equitable quality. Concerns of the burgeoning population of the urban poor are still not reflected in planning. The expectations and aspirations of the poor for education cannot be set aside as being outside the frame of curricular concerns.

The social context of education in India thus presents a number of challenges which must be addressed by the curriculum framework, both in its design as well as its implementation. The discussion on guiding principles has drawn attention to these challenges as well as some of the ways in which they can bc addressed. Opening the concept of knowledge to include new areas of knowledge and experience, inclusivity in selecting learning tasks, pedagogic practices that are alert to promoting participation, building self-confidence and critical awareness, and an openness to engaging with community to explain and share curricular decisions are among the new ideas discussed in different sections of this document.

1.7 AIMS OF EDUCATION

The aims of education serve as broad guidelines to align educational processes to chosen ideals and accepted principles. Aims of education simultaneously reflect the current needs and aspirations of a society as well as lasting values, immediate concerns of a community as well as broad human ideals. At any given time and place they can be called contemporary and contextual articulation of broad and lasting human aspirations and values.

Educational aims turn the different activities undertaken in schools and other educational institutions into a creative pattern and give them a distinguished character of being 'educational'. An educational aim helps the teacher connect her present classroom activity to a cherished future outcome without making it instrumental, and therefore, give it direction without divorcing it from the current concerns. Thus, an aim is a foreseen end: it is not an idle view of a mere spectator; rather, it influences the steps taken to reach the end. An aim must provide foresight. It can do this in three ways: First, it involves careful observation of the given conditions to see what means are available for reaching the end, and to discover the hindrances in the way. This may require careful study of children, and what they are capable of learning at different ages. Second, this foresight suggests the proper order or sequence that would be effective. Third, it makes the choice of alternatives possible. Therefore, acting with an aim allows us to act intelligently. The school, classroom, and related learning sites are spaces where the core of educational activity takes place. These must become spaces where learners have experiences that help them achieve the desired curricular objectives. An understanding of learners, educational aims, the nature of knowledge, and the nature of the school as a social space, can help us arrive at principles to guide classroom practices.

The guiding principles discussed earlier provide the landscape of social values within which we locate our educational aims. The first is a commitment to democratic values of equality, justice, freedom, concern for others' well-being, secularism, respect for human dignity and rights. Education should aim to build a commitment to these values which are based on reason and understanding. The curriculum, therefore, should provide adequate experience and space for dialogue and discourse in the school to build such a commitment in children.

Independence of thought and action points to a capacity of carefully considered, value-based decision making, independently and collectively.

Sensitivity to others' well-being and feelings, together with knowledge and understanding of the world, should form the basis of a rational commitment to values.

Learning to learn and the willingness to unlearn and relearn are important as means of responding to new situations in a flexible and creative manner. The curriculum needs to emphasise the processes of constructing knowledge.

Choices in life and ability to participate in democratic processes depend on the ability to contribute to society in various ways. This is why education must develop the ability to work, participate in economic processes and social change. This necessitates the integration of work with education. We must ensure that work related experiences are sufficient and broad-based in terms of skills and attitudes, an understanding of socio-economic processes, and help inculcate a mental frame to work with others in a spirit of cooperation. Work alone can create a social temper.

Appreciation of beauty and art forms is an integral part of human life. Creativity in arts, literature and other domains of knowledge is closely linked. Education must provide the means and opportunities to enhance the child's creative expression and the capacity of aesthetic appreciation. Education for aesthetic appreciation and creativity is more important today when aesthetic gullibility allows for opinion and taste to be manufactured and manipulated by market forces. The effort should be to enable the learner to appreciate beauty in its several forms. However, we must ensure that we do not promote stereotypes of beauty and forms of entertainment, which might constitute an affront to women and persons with disabilities.

OBSERVATIONS

1.1 Introduction

As usual, the prevailing system of education is criticised. It also refers to the recommendations made in '*Learning without Burden*' (1993). As already stated, the Report by and large, failed to make any work while impact its. Several reforms have been introduced as a follow-up of the Revised NPE-1992. Much water has flown over the river Ganges since the publication of the report.

1.2 Retrospect

Here, a brief summary of the efforts made to restructure the system of education is made. The restrospect ends again with a reference to the Report '*Learning without Burden*'. Nothing substantial is said in this part and it merits no attention.

1.3 National Curriculum Framework

Parrot-like mention is made of the information loaded textbooks. It is not quite correct to state that the textbooks do not provide for creative work and independent thinking. The NCERT books are prepared by the NCERT staff who is supposed to be well-versed with the techniques of writing textbooks. It is usually claimed by the NCERT that its books are of very high quality. Moreover, it is not fair to presume that authors of books published by private publishers are devoid of all understanding as to how children learn. They do take into account the broader aims of education, the social milieu of children, the nature of knowledge in its broader sense, the nature of human development and the process of learning. The three-fourth matter contained in this section is devoted to the observations contained in the NPE, 1986, and the programme of Action (POA), 1992.

1.4 Guiding Principles

These are often repeated principles in all textbooks used by the B.Ed. students.

All aspects of decentralisation and emphasis on the role of Panchayati Raj Institutions have been examined by the Central Advisory Board Committee on Decentralisation of Educational Planning: Panchayati Raj: Veerapan Report (1993).

A regard sensitiveness to environment, a good deal of emphasis already exists in the curriculum.

More than one page is devoted to quotes on democracy from the report of the Secondary Education Commission 1952-53.

1.5 The Quality Dimension

This section refers to the views of late J.P. Naik on the 'elusive triangle' of equality, quality and quantity . It also draws attention to the UNESCO's recently published global monitoring report, however, without mentioning the title of the report. '*The National Curriculum Framework for School Education*' (2000) gave a careful thought to all the issues contained in this section. This section does not throw any fresh light on the issue.

Major recommendations of the UNESCO International Conference on Education held at Geneva, 8-11 September 2004 quality education are given in the Appendix.

Reference is also made to the report of Chattopadhya Commission (1984) on School Teachers.

As regards standards in teacher education, a good deal of work has already been done by the National Council of Teacher Education which has been given a statutory status by the Ministry of HRD (1992). It has published several documents. Mention may be made of the following:

1. *Curriculum Framework for Teacher Education—Discussion Document*, 1996.
2. '*Restructuring and Revitalising Teacher Education*', 1998.

Besides it has fixed norms for establishing different types of teacher education institutions.

A perusal of the expansion of teacher education colleges in the last few years indicates that NCTE has not demonstrated its will to check the mushroom growth.

1.6 The Social Context of Education

No comments are needed as the paragraph very rightly highlights the need to provide increased facilities to the girls belonging to dalit and adivasi communities among the rural and urban areas. It also emphasises that education system should be in the social context.

1.7 Aims of Education

This section sets out the following aims of education:

1. Commitment to democratic values of equality, justice, freedom.
2. Concern for other's well-being.
3. Secularism
4. Respect for human dignity and rights.

The document, however, ignores the following aims:

1. National integration.
2. Vocational aim.
3. Ethical aim.
4. Spiritual aim.
5. National development aim.
6. Service to society.

3

Learning and Knowledge

Learning and Knowledge is the chapter 2 of the draft which is as under with the observations.

This chapter establishes the need to recognise the child as a natural learner, and knowledge as the outcome of the child's own activity. In our everyday lives outside the school, we enjoy the curiosity, inventiveness and constant querying of children. They actively engage with the world around, exploring, responding, inventing and working things out, and making meaning. Childhood is a period of growth and change, involving developing ones physical and mental capacities to the fullest. It involves being socialised into adult society, into acquiring and creating knowledge of the world and oneself in relation to others in order to understand, to act, and to transform. Each new generation inherits the storehouse of culture and knowledge in society by integrating it into one's own web of activities and understanding, and realising its 'fruitfulness' in creating afresh.

2.1 PRIMACY OF THE ACTIVE LEARNER

Informal learning in society builds on learners' the natural capability to draw upon and construct their own knowledge, to develop their capacities, in relating to the environment around, both physical and social, and to the task on hand. For this to happen, opportunities to try out, manipulate, make mistakes and correct oneself are essential. This is as true of learning language as it is of a craft skill or a discipline. Schools as institutions provide new opportunities for all learners to learn about themselves, others, and society, to access their inheritance and engage with it irrespective of and outside the access provided by one's birth into a family and community. The formal processes of learning that school makes possible can open up new possibilities in of understanding and relating to the world.

Our current concern in curriculum to make it an inclusive and meaningful experience for children, alongwith the effort to move away from a textbook culture requires a fundamental change in how we think of learners and the process of learning. Hence the need to engage in detail with the underpinnings and implications of 'childcentred' education.

'Child-centred' pedagogy means giving primacy to children's experiences, their voices, and their active participation. This kind of pedagogy requires us to plan learning in keeping with children's psychological development and interests. The learning plans therefore must respond to physical, cultural and social preferences within the wide diversity of characteristics and needs. Our school pedagogic practices, learning tasks, and the texts we create for learners, tend to focus on the socialisation of children and on the 'receptive' features of children's learning. Instead, we need to nurture and build on their active and creative capabilities—their inherent interest in making meaning, in relating to the world in 'real' ways through acting on it and creating, and in relating to other humans. Learning is active and social in its character. Frequently, the notions of 'good student' that are promoted emphasise obedience to the teacher, moral character, and acceptance of the teacher's words as 'authoritative' knowledge.

2.2 LEARNERS IN CONTEXT

Children's voices and experiences do not find expression in the classroom—often the only voice heard is that of the teacher when children speak, they are usually only answering the teacher's questions or repeating the teacher's words. They rarely do things, nor do they have opportunities to take initiative. The curriculum must enable children to find their voices, nurture their curiosity—to do things, to ask questions and to pursue investigations, sharing and integrating their experiences with school knowledge—rather than their ability to reproduce textual knowledge. Reorienting the curriculum to this end must be among our highest priorities, informing the preparation of teachers, the annual plans of schools, the design of textbooks, learning materials and teaching plans, and evaluation and examination patterns.

Children will learn only in an atmosphere where they feel they are valued. Our schools still do not convey this to *all* children. The association of learning with fear, discipline and stress, rather than enjoyment and satisfaction is detrimental to learning. Our children need to feel that each one of them, their homes, communities, languages and cultures, are valuable; that their diverse capabilities are accepted; that all of them have the ability and the right to learn and to access knowledge and skills;

and that adult society regards them as capable of the best. We are becoming better aware of the importance of these needs as our schools expand and increasingly include children from all sections of society. The mid-day meal and the provisioning of infrastructural support and pedagogic concern for inclusive education are among the most significant developments in recent times. A strong stand must be taken against all forms of corporal punishment. The boundaries of the school need to become more porous to the community. At the same time, the problems of curriculum load and examination-related stress require urgent attention in all their dimensions. Physical and emotional security is the cornerstone for all learning, right from the primary to the secondary school years, and even afterwards.

2.3 DEVELOPMENT AND LEARNING

The period from infancy to adolescence is one of rapid growth and change. The curriculum must have a holistic approach to learning and development that is able to see the interconnections and transcend divisions between physical and mental development, and between individual development and interaction with others.

2.3.1 The precondition for all development is healthy physical growth of all children. This adequate nutrition, physical exercise and freedom from all forms of physical discomfort.

Free-play, informal and formal games and sports activities are essential to the physical development of children, while also providing them with leisure time to de-stress. The range of abilities include stamina, fine and gross motor skills and dexterities, self-awareness and control, and coordination in team games. Simple adaptation of equipment and rules can make all such activities and games inclusive so that children with physical impairments can also participate along with others. Children can achieve high levels of excellence in sports, athletics, gymnastics, yoga and performing arts such as dance. When the emphasis shifts from enjoyment to achievement, such training can make demands of discipline and practice which can create stress at this stage.

Physical development supports mental and cognitive development, especially in young children. The capacity to think, reason and make sense of the self and the world, and to use language, is intimately connected with acting and interacting—doing things by oneself and with others.

2.3.2 Cognition involves the capacity to make sense of the self and the world, through action and language. Meaningful learning is a generative process, of representing and manipulating concrete things and mental representations, rather than storage and retrieval of information. Thinking, language (verbal or sign) and doing things are thus intimately inter-twined. This is a process that begins at infancy, and develops through independent and mediated activities. Initially children are cognitively oriented to the here and now, able to reason and act logically on concrete experiences. As their linguistic capabilities and their ability to work in the company of others develops, it opens up possibilities of more complex reasoning in tasks that involve abstraction, planning and dealing with ends that are not in view. There is overall increasing capability of working with the hypothetical, and reasoning in the world of the possible.

Conceptual development is thus a continuous process of deepening and enriching connections and acquiring new layers of meaning. Alongside is the development of theories that children have about the natural and social worlds, including themselves in relation to others, which provide them with explanations for why things are the way they are, the relationships between causes and effects, and the bases for decisions and acting. Attitudes, emotions and morals are thus integral an part of cognitive development, and are linked to the development of language, mental representations, concepts and reasoning. As children's metacognitive capabilities develop, they become more aware of their own beliefs and capable of regulating their own learning.

- All children are naturally motivated to learn and are capable of learning.
- Making meaning, and developing the capacity for abstract thinking, reflection and work are the most important aspects of learning.
- Children learn in a variety of ways—through experience, making and doing things, experimentation, reading, discussion, asking, listening, thinking and reflecting, and expressing oneself in speech, movement or writing—both individually and with others. They require opportunities of all these kinds in the course of their development. Children with disabilities especially require multisensorial experiences to support conceptual development.
- Teaching something before the child is cognitively ready takes away from learning it at a later stage. Children may 'remember' many facts but they may not understand them or be able to relate them to the world around.
- Learning takes place both within school and outside school. Learning is enriched if the two arenas interact with each other. Art and work provide opportunities for holistic learning rich in

tacit and aesthetic components. Such experiences are essential for linguistically known things especially in moral and ethical matters, to be learnt through direct experience, and integrated into life.

- Learning must be paced so that it allows learners to engage with concepts and deepen understanding, rather than remembering only to forget after examinations. Children with disabilities often need more time to repeat in order to learn. At the same time learning must provide variety and challenge, and be interesting and engaging. Boredom is a sign that the task may have become mechanically repetitive for the child and of little cognitive value.
- Learning can take place with or without mediation. In the case of the latter, the social context and interactions, especially with more capable others, provide avenues for learners to work at cognitive levels above their own.

2.3.3 Adolescence is a critical period for development of self identity. Acquiring a sense of self and one's own physical body are interlinked. The physical space of the outside world, one's access to it and free movement influence construction of the self. This is of special significance in the case of girls who are often constrained by social conventions to stay indoors. These very conventions promote the opposite stereotype for boys which associates them with outdoors and physical process. These stereotypes get especially heightened during the biological maturational changes of adolescence. It is a time when the given and internalised norms and ideas are questioned, while at the same time opinions of others and the peer group become very important. Children need social and emotional support during this period, to develop a comfortable relationship with themselves and the way they look and relate to others, especially the opposite sex. The absence of such support can lead to confusion and misunderstanding about these changes and also to giving up sports and outdoor activities.

It is important that identities of gender, class, caste, religion and minority status, or those rooted in physical impairments do not constrain participation in the experiences provided in school. Unfortunately, this is presently often the case. Children need to progressively learn the distinction between conventions and moral or ethical principles. Such reasoning cannot itself ensure ethical behaviour. Opportunities to discuss and reflect on moral dilemmas are essential to produce a change in ethical reasoning, along with greater self-reflection in interacting with others and with society in general.

Personal identity and ethics are to be developed and negotiated with reference to the current social context. Rather than 'mainstreaming' there is need today to encourage and support the development of plural identities along with one's identity as being Indian, bounded by a universal culture of rationality, mutual respect and peace.

2.3.4 'Learning Disabilities' is a functional term that is being used to refer to a heterogeneous group of 'disorders' reflected in what is seen as 'underachievement' in listening, speaking, reading, writing, reasoning and mathematics. These are believed to be consequences of a dysfunction of the central nervous system. This term does not apply to children with sensory impairments, whose learning is normal but different—constrained in some facets by the impairment, and enhanced in other sensory dimensions.

While learning disabilities may occur along with other problems in sensory impairments, mental retardation and social, emotional or environmental disturbances, they are also seen to result from insufficient or inappropriate instruction. In practice however, the diagnostic criteria are not well established. There is inadequate research on understanding causes, diagnosis and treatment, and the set of possible causes are rarely systematically evaluated There is also growing controversy regarding the extent to which underachievement of children may be of pedagogical origin. Notions such as 'learning disability' tend to reduce difficulties that children may face in school, because they come from different socio-cultural backgrounds or are first generation school goers, to individual attributes and dysfunctions. In spite of these issues, the idea of testing for learning difficulties or disabilities and conducting remediation for the same, in all subjects and for all class grades, is gaining acceptance and tests are now being routinely prescribed in many states. This is reason for concern as where there are learning disabilities, simplistic measures to be devised routinely by teachers cannot be the answer. Research, specialised diagnostic testing and individually planned remediation programmes are necessary. In the absence of such inputs, it only creates 'labels' for children.

2.4 IMPLICATIONS FOR CURRICULUM AND PRACTICE

2.4.1 Teaching for Construction of Knowledge

The teachers' own role in children's cognition could be enhanced if they assume a more active role in relation to process of knowledge construction in which children are engaged. A child constructs her/his knowledge while engaged in the process of learning. Allowing children to ask questions, that require them to relate what they are learning in school to things happening outside, encouraging children to answer in their own words and from their own experiences, rather than simply memorising and getting answers right in just one way—all these are small but important steps in helping children develop their understanding. 'Intelligent guessing' must be encouraged as a valid pedagogic tool. Quite often children have an idea arising from their everyday experiences, or because of their exposure to the media, but they are not quite ready to articulate it in ways that a teacher might appreciate it. It is in this 'zone' between what you know and what you almost know that new knowledge is constructed. Such knowledge often takes the form of skills, which are cultivated outside the school, at home or in the community. All such forms of knowledge and skills must be respected. A sensitive and informed teacher is aware of this and is able to engage children through well chosen tasks and questions, so that they are able to realise their developmental potential.

Active engagement involves enquiry, exploration, questioning, debates, application and reflection leading to theory building and creation of ideas/positions. Schools must provide opportunities to question, enquire, debate, reflect, and arrive at concepts or create new ideas. An element of challenge is critical for the process of active engagement and learning various concepts, skills and positions through the process. What is challenging for a particular age-group becomes easy and uninteresting for the other age group, and may be remote and uninteresting at another stage.

So often, in the name of 'objectivity', teachers sacrifice flexibility and creativity. Very often teachers, in government as well as private schools, insist that all children must give identical answers to questions. The argument given for not accepting other answers is that "they cannot give answers that are not there in the textbook."; we discussed it in the staff room and decided that we will only accept this answer as right!", or that "there will be too many types of answers, then should we accept them all?"

Such arguments make a travesty of the meaning of learning and only serve to convince children and parents that schools are irrationally rigid. We must indeed, contemplate why we only ask children to *give* answers to questions. Even the ability to make a set of questions for given answers is a valid test of learning.

2.4.2 The Value of Interactions

Learning takes place through interactions with the environment around, nature, things and people, both through actions and through language. Physical activity of moving, exploration and doing things, on ones own, with one's peers or in the company of adults, using language—to read, to express or ask, to listen and to interact, are the key processes through which learning occurs. The context in which learning takes place is thus of direct cognitive significance.

Much of our school learning is still individual based (although not individualised!) The teacher is seen as transmitting 'knowledge' – which is usually confused with information to children, and organising experiences in order to help children learn. But interactions with teachers, with other peers of the same age group, as well as those who are older and younger can open up many more rich learning possibilities. Learning in the company of others is a process of interacting with each other and also through the learning task on hand. This kind of learning gets enriched when schools enrol children from different socio-economic backgrounds.

In the early primary school years a beginning has been made in the area of group work. Projects and activities that can be carried out by groups need to become a feature of learning in the middle and high school also. There are ways in which such group learning can be assessed and evaluated. Schools could also consider giving mixed age groups of children projects to do together. In such mixed groups there is much that children can learn from each other such as team work and social values. In the company of others, one has opportunities to participate in larger tasks where one may find a niche to contribute to achieving something above one's own potential and one may be able to try out what one does not fully know. Group learning tasks, taking responsibility, and contributing to a task on hand are all important facets of not only acquiring knowledge but also in learning of crafts and arts. In multi-grade class situation, such vertical grouping, which cuts across different grades, and which allows a single activity to be used across age-groups, could provide a pedagogically feasible, sound curriculum plan.

2.4.3 Designing Learning Experiences

The quality of the learning task influences its learnability and its value for the learner. Tasks that are too easy or too difficult, that are repetitive and mechanical, that are based on recalling the text, that do not permit selfexpression and questioning by the child and depend solely on the teacher for correction, make the child assume the passive stance of obedience. Learners learn not to value their own ability to think and reason, that knowledge is created by others and they must only receive it. The onus falls on the teacher to 'motivate' children who do not seem to be naturally motivated. Learners accept being controlled and learn to want to control. These are ultimately detrimental to the growth of cognitive self-reflexivity and flexibility which are essential if learning is to empower the learner. By the time they reach class seven, many children who have grown up in this kind of learning environment, lose their confidence in themselves and their ability to express themselves or make meaning out of their experiences in school. They repeatedly resort to mechanical rote memorisation to pass examinations.

Instead, tasks that are challenging and allow independent thinking, and multiple ways of being solved, encourage independence, creativity and self-discipline in learners. Instead of a culture of quizzing, of answering quickly and always knowing the right answer, we need to allow learners to spend time on deeper meaningful learning.

Learning tasks that are designed to ensure that children will be encouraged to seek out knowledge from sites other than the textbook, in their own experience, in the experiences of people at home and in the community, in libraries and other sites outside the school, communicate the philosophy that learning and knowledge are to be sought out, authenticated and thereby constructed, and that neither the textbook nor the teacher is an authority. In this context, heritage sites assume great significance as sites of learning. Not just the history teacher, but teachers of all subjects need to inculcate in the children under their care a sense of respect for sites of archaeological significance and the desire to explore and understand their significance.

There have been efforts towards improving the classroom environment and curriculum planning for children in classes I and II in recent years. While these need to be reviewed and strengthened, there is also need to engage with questions of designing learning experiences for older children that help them understand concepts and create and 'own' the knowledge they learn. We are now seeing a small shift away the focus on 'factual knowledge', but teacher preparation, planning of classroom practice, textbook preparation, and evaluation need to support this shift more decisively. There is need to realise flexibility in planning, and adapting textbooks content to designing topic learning, so as to move towards the NPE-86 goal of breaking out of watertight compartments. For this it is necessary to build the capabilities and confidence in teachers to autonomously plan their teaching in response to children's learning. Currently pedagogic reform efforts are still very centralised. Effective decentralisation would be possible through the greater involvement of Cluster and Block Resource Centres, the availability of local resource persons, and of resource and reference materials for teachers to use.

2.4.4 Approaches to Planning

Our educational practice is still based on limited 'lesson plans' aimed at achieving measurable 'behaviours'; in this view the child is akin to a creature that can be trained, or a computer that can be programmed. Hence, there is too much focus on 'outcomes', and presenting knowledge into bits of information to be memorised directly from the text or through activities after 'motivating' children, and finally on evaluating to see if children remember! Instead. we need to view the child as 'constructing knowledge', all the time. This is true not only for 'cognitive subjects' such as mathematics and science, language and social science, but equally of values, skills and attitudes.

This perspective on the learner may sound 'obvious', but in fact, many teachers, evaluators, and textbook writers still lack conviction that this can become a reality.

- The term 'activity' is now a part of the register of most elementary school teachers, but in many cases this has just been grafted onto the 'Herbartian' lesson plan, still driven by 'outcomes' at the end of each lesson. There is now more talk of competencies, but these competencies are still pegged onto lessons much in the manner of 'outcomes'. Instead teachers need to develop the ability to plan 'units' of four or five sessions for each topic. The development of understanding and of competencies is also possible only through repeated opportunities to use the competencies in different situation, and in a variety of ways. While development of knowledge, understanding and skills can be assessed both at the end of a unit, and revisited at a later date, assessment cycle for competencies needs to be longer.
- Activities could enable teachers to give individualised attention to children, and to make alternations in a task depending on their requirements and variations in interest. In fact, teachers could also consider involving children and older learners in planning the class work—such variety would bring tremendous richness to the classroom processes. It would also allow teachers to respond to children with special needs and those in need of greater attention, without making it seem as if it is an obvious exception. There is still not enough engagement of the teacher with the learning of each child—children are treated en-masse, and only those who are regarded 'stars' or 'problematic' are noticed. All children would benefit from such attention.
- A lesson plan or unit plan for a class where there are children with special needs and children with learning difficulties should indicate how the teacher alters the on-going activity for them. Failure to learn is currently being mechanically addressed

through 'remediation', which usually means simply repeating lessons for these children. Many teachers are also looking for 'cures' to set right the problems that these children have. They still find it difficult to individualise learning for such children, based on building upon what they are able to do.

- Teachers need to understand how to plan lessons so that children are challenged to think and to try out what they are learning, and not simply repeat what is told to them. A new problem is that in the name of 'activities' and 'play way' methods, a lot of learning is being diluted by giving children things to do that are far below their capability. One concern is that a focus on activities would become too time consuming and make greater demands on teachers time. Certainly doing activities requires that time be spent in planning and preparing for activities. Initially teachers need to make an effort to establish the classroom culture for activities and to establish the rules that will govern the space and use of materials.
- The practice of teachers in classrooms, the materials they use and the evaluation techniques employed must be internally consistent with each other.

2.4.5 Critical Pedagogy

Teacher and student engagement is critical in the classroom because it has the power to define whose knowledge will become a part of school-related knowledge and whose voices will shape it. Students are not just young people for whom adults should devise solutions. They are critical observers of their own conditions and needs and should be participants in discussions and problem-solving related to their education and future opportunities. Hence children need to be aware that their experiences and perceptions are important and be encouraged to develop their mental skills needed to think and reason independently and have the courage to dissent. What children learn out of school – their capacities, learning abilities, and knowledge base – and bring to school is important to further enhance the learning process. This is all the more critical for children from underprivileged backgrounds, especially girls, as the worlds they inhabit and their realities are underrepresented in school knowledge.

Participatory learning and teaching, emotion and experience need to have a definite and valued place in the classroom. While participation is a powerful strategy, it loses it pedagogic edge when it is ritualised, or merely becomes an instrument to enable teachers to meet their own ends. True participation starts from experiences of both students and teachers.

When children and teachers share and reflect on their individual and collective experiences without fear of judgment, it gives them opportunities to learn about others who may not be a part of their own social reality. This enables them to understand and relate to differences instead of fearing them. If children's social experiences are to be brought into classrooms, it is inevitable that issues of conflict be addressed. Conflict is an inescapable part of children's lives. They constantly encounter situations which call for moral assessment and action, whether in relation to subjective experiences of conflict involving the self, family and society, or in dealing with exposure to violent conflict in the contemporary world. To use conflict as a pedagogic strategy is to enable children to deal with conflict and facilitate awareness of its nature and role in their lives.

Learning to 'read against the grain', to critically question received knowledge, whether it is in the 'biased' textbook, or other literary sources in their own environments, can be built by encouraging learners to comment, compare and think about elements that exist in their own environment. Women and dalit educators have used songs as a powerful medium for discussion, comment and analysis. As repositories of knowledge exist in different mediums, all these forms whether television, advertisements, songs, paintings etc. need to be brought in to create a dynamic interaction between learners themselves.

A pedagogy that is sensitive to gender, class, caste and global inequalities is one that does not merely affirm different individual and collective experiences but locates these within larger structures of power and raises questions such as who is allowed to speak for whom? Whose knowledge is most valued? This requires evolving differing strategies for different learners. For example encouraging speaking in class may be important for some children, while for others it may be learning to listen to others.

The role of teachers is to provide a safe space for children to express themselves and simultaneously to build in certain forms of interactions. They need to step out of the role of 'moral authority' and learn to listen with empathy and without judgment, and to enable children to listen to each other. While consolidating and constructively stretching the limits of the learner's understanding they need to be conscious of how differences are expressed. An atmosphere of trust would make the classroom a safe space where children can share experiences, where conflict can be acknowledged and constructively questioned, and where resolutions, however tentative, can be mutually worked out. In particular, for girls and children from under priviledged social groups, schools and classrooms should be spaces to discuss processes of decision-making, to question the basis of their decisions and to make informed choices.

2.5 KNOWLEDGE AND UNDERSTANDING

The question 'what should be taught to the young'? derives from a deeper question, namely 'what aims are worth pursuing' in education—a vision of the capabilities and values that every individual must have and a sociopolitical and cultural vision for society. This is not a single aim, but a set of aims. So also, the content selected seeks to do justice to the entire set of aims: it has to be comprehensive and balanced. The curriculum needs to provide experiences that build the knowledge base through a progressive introduction to the capabilities of thinking rationally, to understand the world through the disciplines, aesthetic appreciation, and sensitivity to others, to work and to participate in economic processes. This section discusses the nature and forms of knowledge and understanding as necessary terrains for making informed curricular choices and approaches to content.

Knowledge can be conceived as experience organised, through language, into patterns of thought (or structures of concepts), thus creating meaning, which in turn helps understand the world we live in. It can also be conceived of as patterns of activity, or physical dexterity with thought, contributing to acting in the world, creating and making of things. Human beings, over time, have evolved both a wealth of **bodies of knowledge** which includes a repertoire of **ways of thinking, of feeling and of doing things** and constructing more knowledge. All children have to re-create a significant part of this wealth for themselves, as this is important as the basis for further thinking and for acting appropriately in this world. It is also important to learn to participate in the very process of knowledge creation, meaning making and human action, *i.e.* work. Conceiving knowledge in this broad sense directs us to the importance of examining knowledge in terms of not only the 'product', but also the underlying principles of how it is created, how it is organised, who accesses it, and what it is used for. It suggests that in the curriculum, there must be as much focus on the process of learning, on how learners engage with and reconstruct knowledge, as on the content of what is learnt.

If, on the other hand, knowledge is regarded as a finished product, then it is organised in the form of information to be 'transferred' to the child's mind. Education would concern itself with maintaining and transmitting this store-house of human knowledge. In this view of knowledge, the learner is conceived of as a passive receiver, while in the former there is a dynamic engagement with the world through observing, feeling, reflecting, acting, and sharing.

Curriculum is a plan to develop capabilities that are likely to help achieve the chosen educational aims. The range of human capabilities is very wide, and through education we cannot develop them all. The concern is therefore with those that are necessary and significant in relation to our aims, which offer potential for further development, and for which we have some pedagogic knowledge.

2.5.1 Basic Capabilities

Children's basic capabilites are those that form the broad basis for the development of understanding, values and skills.

(a) **Language** and other forms of expression provide the basis for meaning making, and sharing with others. They create possibilities of development of understanding and knowledge, providing the ability to symbolise, codify and to remember and record. Development of language for a child is synonymous with development of understanding and identity and also the capability to relate with others. Not only verbal languages with scripts, but also languages without scripts, sign languages, scripts such as Braille and performing arts provide the bases for making meaning and expression.

(b) **Forming and sustaining relationships** with the social world, with the natural world, and with one's self, with emotional richness, sensitivity and values. This gives meaning to life, providing it with emotional content and purpose. This is also the basis for ethics and morality.

(c) **Capabilities for work and action**, involves the coordination of bodily movement with thought and volition; drawing on skill and understanding and directing to achieve some purpose or create something. It also involves handling tools and technologies, to manipulate and organise things and experiences, and to communicate.

2.5.2 Knowledge in Practice

A vast array of human activities, excellences and modes of activity sustain social living and culture. Crafts such as weaving, carpentry and pottery, occupations such as farming and shop keeping constitute alongwith various kinds of performing and visual arts and sport a valuable form of knowledge. These forms of knowledge are of a practical nature, tacit and often only partially articulated.

Many of them involve abilities that are developed. These include the ability to conceptualise and imagine products that are useful or aesthetic, the knowledge of and ability to work with materials to fashion the product, knowledge of one's own abilities, team work and attitudes of persistence and discipline. This is true whether it is an object being fashioned or a production to be presented to an audience.

Describing these activities as skills draws attention to only the dexterities that are involved, but not to the considerable understanding of the social and natural world and the self, that each of these forms of practice involves. Like accepted academic disciplines these crafts and trades too have their traditions and expert practitioners. The knowledge relevant to each of these crafts, occupations and art forms—cumulatively develop and are passed on through experience and reflection to the next generation of practitioners. Therefore each one of them is a discipline of practical knowledge. The Indian heritage of such forms of practical knowledge is vast, varied and rich. As productive skills they are an invaluable part of the economy.

More reflection and research is needed in order to understand the epistemological structure of these practical disciplines. Understanding how they practiced and learnt, and how to formalise their learning, are questions of sociological import as traditional occupations are linked to caste groups and are gendered. It is necessary to realise their curricular significance, not only as forms of work but equally as forms of knowledge, and as medium for other learning. This important area of human knowledge needs to become a substantial part of the school curriculum.

2.5.3 Forms of Understanding

Knowledge can be categorised based on distinct kinds of concepts and meanings involved and processes of validation and justification. Each involves its own kind of kind of 'critical thinking', its own way of verifying and authenticating knowledge and its own kind of 'creativity'.

Mathematics has its own distinctive concepts, such as prime number, square root, fraction, integral and function. It also has its own validation procedure, namely a step-by-step demonstration of the necessity of what is to be established. The validation procedures of mathematics are never empirical, never based on observation of the world or on experiment, but are demonstrations, internal to the system specified by the appropriate set of axioms and definitions.

The *natural sciences*, like the systems of mathematics, have their own concepts, often interconnected through theories, and are attempts to describe and explain the natural world. Concepts include atom, magnetic field, cell, and neurone. Scientific inquiry involves observation and experimentation to validate predictions made by theory (hypotheses), which may be aided by instruments and controls. Formalisation into theory and model building can sometimes involve mathematics but it only with reference to observations and not to mathematical accuracy that truth is tested. The attempt is to furnish a narrative which in some way 'corresponds' to reality.

Social sciences have their own concepts, for example community, modernisation, culture, identity, and polity. The social sciences concern themselves with description, explanation and prediction in the social world. The social sciences' hypotheses are about the human behaviour in collective living, and their validation finally depends on the observations made in the society.

With regard to the process of knowledge formation, the natural and social sciences are almost identical. But there are two differences that are of great relevance in curriculum planning. First, the social sciences study human behaviour which is governed by 'reasons', while the nature is governed by 'cause-effect'. Second, findings of social sciences often raise issues of ethics and desirability while natural phenomena can be understood, raising ethical questions only when they enter into the domain of human action.

History is distinct from the social sciences and indeed from mathematic and science in that it is an attempt to construct, on the basis of such evidences as survive, a narrative of particular human actions and activities. Since it is the actions and activities of humans that is described, the concept of human motivation rather than specially constructed theoretical concepts give much of the meaning to the narrative. The establishment of 'the facts' is a process inseparable from the construction of the narrative.

Art and aesthetics use quite familiar words, such as rhythm, harmony, expression and balance, though giving them new senses or new ranges of application. Art productions cannot be judged against reality or for 'truth'. Although there is ample scope for subjective judgement in art, yet it is also possible to educate the artistic imagination to critically judge what is good and what is not.

Ethics is concerned with all human values, and with the rules, principles, standards and ideals which give them expression. In relation to action and choice, therefore, ethics must be conceded primacy over each of the forms of understanding. Ethical understanding involves understanding reasons for judgments—for what makes some things and some acts right and others wrong—regardless of the authority of the persons involved. Furthermore, such reasons will be reasons for anyone; reason, equality and personal autonomy are therefore very intimately connected concepts.

Philosophy involves a concern on the one hand, with analytical clarification, evaluation and synthetic coordination of the afore mentioned forms of understanding in relation to life, and, on the other hand with the whole, the ultimate meaning and the transcendent.

The basic capabilities, the knowledge of practice and the forms of understanding are the core ways in which human experience has, been elaborated in the course of history. All but the simplest kinds of human activity draw upon them—the liberal professions, technologies, industry and commerce. They are central to human culture. Imagination and critical thinking are linked in obvious ways with the development of understanding and reason, and so are the emotions.

Each of these knowledge areas involves a special vocabulary, concepts, theories, descriptions and methodologies. Each provides a 'lens' through which to view the world, to understand, engage, and act in it. These areas have developed, and continue to grow, through the contributions of people in the past. They have also changed in their structure and emphasis, A variety of intelligences and forms of knowing come into play while learning these areas: 'formal modes' of explicit reasoning and articulation, looking for and evaluating evidence, 'experiential', tacit knowing through doing and undergoing the experience, coordinating, observing, and 'practical' engagement, by one-self or in coordination with others, to make or accomplish something, to address problems and issues while charting a course of action. Creativity and excellence are integral to all these forms of knowledge and knowing.

This accumulation of human culture and knowledge, and ways of knowing and doing things, is a valuable part of the inheritance of human society. All our children have a right to access this knowledge, to educate and enrich their commonsense to develop and discover themselves and the world of nature and people, through these lenses and tools.

2.6 RECREATING KNOWLEDGE

These capabilities, practices, and skills of understanding are what we seek to develop through the school curriculum. Some of them, readily lend themselves to being formulated as 'subjects' of study such as mathematics, history, natural sciences, and visual arts. Others, such as ethical understanding, need to be interwoven into subjects and activities. The basic capabilities of language require both approaches, while aesthetic understanding readily lends itself to both approaches. All these areas require opportunities for project activities, thematic and inter-disciplinary courses of studies, field trips, use of libraries and laboratories.

This approach to knowledge necessitates a move away from 'facts' as ends in themselves, to locating facts in the process through which they come to be known, and moving below the surface of facts to the deeper connections between them which give them meaning and significance.

In India we have traditionally followed a subject based approach to organising the curriculum, drawing on only the disciplines. This approach tends to present knowledge as 'packaged' usually in textbooks, along with associated rituals of examinations to assess, and marks as a way of judging competence in the subject area. This approach has led to several problems in our education system. First, those areas that do not lend themselves to being organised in textbooks and examined through marks become sidelined and described as 'extra' or 'cocurricular', instead of being an integral part of the curriculum. These rarely receive the attention they deserve in terms of preparation of teachers or school time. Areas of knowledge such as crafts and sports, which are rich in potential for the development of skill, aesthetics, creativity, resourcefulness and capabilities for team work, also become sidelined. Important areas of knowledge such as work, and associated practical intelligences, have been completely neglected, and we still do not have an adequate curriculum theory to support the development of knowledge, skills and attitudes in these areas.

Second, the subject areas tend to become water tight compartments. As a result, knowledge seems fragmented rather than inter-related and integrated. The discipline, rather than the child's way of viewing the world tends to become the starting point and boundaries get constructed between knowledge in the school and knowledge outside.

Third, what is already known gets emphasised subverting children's own ability to construct knowledge and explore novel ways of knowing. Information takes precedence over knowledge, lending itself to producing bulky textbooks, 'quizzing' and mechanical retrieval rather than understanding and problem solving. This tendency of mistaking information for knowledge leads to 'loading' the curriculum with too many facts to be remembered.

Fourth, there is the issue of including 'new subjects'. The need for subjects to address contemporary concerns of society is important. But there has been a misplaced tendency to address these concerns in the school curriculum by 'creating' new subjects, producing related textbooks and devising methods of evaluation for them. These concerns may be far better addressed if they are incorporated in the curriculum through existing subjects and ongoing activities. Needless to say, adding new areas as 'subjects' only increases curriculum load, and perpetuates undesirable compartmentalisation of knowledge.

Finally, the principles for selecting knowledge for inclusion in the curriculum are not well worked out. There is insufficient consideration of developmental appropriateness, logical sequencing and connection between different grades, and overall pacing, with a few or no opportunities to return to earlier concepts. Further, concepts that cut across subject areas, such as in secondary school mathematics and in physics, are not placed in relation to one another.

2.7 CHILDREN'S KNOWLEDGE AND LOCAL KNOWLEDGE

The child's community and local environment form the primary context in which learning takes place, and in which knowledge acquires its significance. It is in interaction with the environment that the child constructs knowledge derives meaning. Although this area has generally been neglected both in conceptualisation of textbooks, and in pedagogic practices. Hence in this document, we emphasise the significance of contextualizing education: of situating learning in child's context, and of making a porous boundary between the school and its natural and social environment. This is not only because the local environment and the child's own experiences is the best 'entry point' into the study of disciplines of knowledge, but more so because *knowledge is to connect with the world.* It is not a means to an end, but both means and end. This does not require us to reduce knowledge to the functional and immediately relevant but to realise its dynamism by connecting with the world through it.

Unless learners can locate their individual standpoints in relation to the contexts represented in textbooks and relate this knowledge to their experiences of society, knowledge is reduced to the level of mere information. If we want to examine how learning relates to future visions of community life, it is crucial to encourage reflection on *what it means to know something*, and how to use what we have learnt. The learner must be recognised as a proactive participant in his or her own learning.

Day after day children bring to school their experiences of the world around—the trees that they have climbed, the fruits they have eaten, the birds they have tried admire. All children are alive to the natural cycles of day and night, of the weather, the water, the plants and the animals that surround them. Children, when they enter class I already have a rich language base, of small numbers and the rudiments of operations already in place. Yet, rarely do we head the knowledge that they already have which they bring into the classroom. Rarely do we ask children to talk about or refer the world outside the school during our lessons and teaching. Instead we resort to the convenience of the printed word and pictures of the rich natural environment, all of which are poor replicas of the natural world. Worse still, today in the name of computer-aided learning, the living world is being turned into animation strips that children are expected to watch on their computer screens. Before starting a lesson on living and non-living, if a teacher were to take her class out on a walk through the field near the school, and on returning and each child to write the names of ten living things and ten non living things that she saw, results would be amazing. Children in Mahabalipuram in Tamil Nadu, may include in their list things sea shell, pebbles and fish, and those in Chhatisgarh near the Dandakaranya forest may include nest, bee hive, and anklet. Instead, children are usually required to look at a drawing in the textbook, or a list of words, and sort the things out as living and nonliving. During the lesson on water pollution, children could examine the water sources and water bodies in their local areas and then connect it with types of pollution. Instead, they are expected to see pictures of polluted water, and comment on them. When studying the moon and its phases, how many teachers actually ask the children to look at the moon at night and then talk about it the next day? Instead of asking children the names of local birds and trees, our textbooks name 'ubiquitous' things that seem to belong everywhere and yet belong nowhere. Only if children in say class VIII can connect the chapter on photosynthesis with the real plants around, would they think of asking questions such as 'how do crotons which have coloured leaves with no green leaves manage to manufacture their own food?'. Only when the living world around becomes available for critical reflection within the school, would they become alive to issues of the environment and nurture their concern for it.

The local is thus a natural learning resource that must be priviledged while making choices regarding what should be included, what concrete examples should be cited in planning for their transaction in the classroom. It also means that the local context may suggest that some concepts are more important than others. This does not mean that only local things can be discussed in the classroom. But when children living in Kerala are introduced to the habitat of the desert in Rajasthan, the descriptions must be rich so that they can get a feel of the natural world there, in its particularities and diversity, rather than the typical sand dune and the camel. They should wonder how in a place so hot, people wear more rather than less clothes. They should also be able to compare life there with life around them in their local community, and ask what things would happen in the same way, and what things would happen differently.

The local environment is not only the physical and natural world but also the socio-cultural world. All children have a voice at home and it is essential for the school to ensure that their voices continue to be heard in the classroom as well. Communities also have rich linguistic resources: local stories, songs, jokes and riddles and art, all of which can enrich language and knowledge in schools. They also have rich oral histories. By imposing silence we stifle children.

2.8 SCHOOL KNOWLEDGE AND THE COMMUNITY

Experiences of the socio-cultural world also need to become a part of curriculum. Children need to find expression and representation of the plurality of peoples and ways of life represented in the textbooks. These portrayals need to ensure that no community is oversimplified, labeled, or judged. It may even be better for children to study and generate portrayals of the local social groups as a part of their social science studies. They can then directly interact with the gram panchayat representative who may have been invited to the school and speak about the extent to which decentralisation has helped in addressing local civic issues. Local oral history could also be connected with regional history and national history. But the social context also calls for a much greater critical awareness and critical engagement on the part of curriculum developers and teachers. Community-based identities of gender, caste, class and religion are primary identities but they can also be oppressive and reaffirm social inequalities and hierarchies. School knowledge can also provide a lens through which children can develop a critical understanding of their social reality. It could also provide them space to talk about their experiences and anxieties within their homes.

Communities may also have questions about the inclusion or exclusion of particular knowledge and experiences in the school curriculum. The school must then be prepared to engage with communities to listen to their concerns, and to persuade them to see the educational value of such decisions. For this teachers must know the reasons why something is included while something else is not. They must also be able to win the trust of parents in matters like allowing children to use home language in school, or teaching about sexuality and reproduction, or play-way methods in primary school or encouraging boys to sing and dance. It is not a good enough explanation to say that the decisions were taken at the State level. If we are to ensure participation of children of all groups in our secular education, we will have to discuss our curricular choices with others who are legitimate stakeholders in education.

2.9 SOME DEVELOPMENTAL CONSIDERATIONS

Children's interests, physical skills, linguistic capacity, and abilities for abstraction and generalisation develop over the span of schooling, from the pre-school period through higher secondary school. This is a period of intensive growth and development and also of fundamental shifts and changes in interests and capabilities. Hence, it is an important dimension of determining the approach to, and the selection and organisation of areas, of the curriculum.

The creation or re-creation of knowledge requires an experiential base, language abilities, and interaction with other humans and the natural world. Children entering school for the first time have already begun constructing knowledge of the world. Everything they learn later will be in relation to this knowledge they bring into the school. This knowledge is also intuitive. School provides opportunities to build on this in a more conscious and engaged manner. At the early stage of learning, from pre-school to the primary school years, an important place must be given to language and mathematics in all activities across the curriculum. The division into subjects is not very significant, and the knowledge areas discussed above can be totally integrated and presented to children in the form of learning experiences of environment. This should include rich interaction with the natural and social environment, understanding, working with one's hands, of social interactions, and developing one's aesthetic capabilities. These early integrated experiences of the natural and social environment would later become demarcated into science and social sciences in the middle school years.

Upper primary or middle school period may be the place for emergence of better defined subject areas taking into consideration the above mentioned forms of knowledge. At this stage it should be possible to create spaces across subjects in which children engage in the process of data collection, natural, social, mathematical or linguistic, to classify and categorise, and also analyse the same through certain knowledge areas such as ethical understanding and critical thinking. The creation of a space for explorations into social issues and knowledge without boundaries could at this stage go a long way in encouraging rational thinking.

By the time children reach the secondary stage of education, they have acquired sufficient knowledge base, experience, language abilities and maturity to engage with different forms of knowledge in their full sense: concepts, structure of body of knowledge, investigation methods and validation procedures. Therefore, the subjects could be more closely linked with the basic forms as listed above and the disciplines as they are recognised in higher education today.

The issues of adequate representation of all forms of knowledge and emphasis on similarities, special characteristics, and widest possible inter connections between them become important when the subjects areas are more clearly defined.

OBSERVATIONS

All the standard books on Educational Psychology provide insight on the learning process. There is nothing in this chapter which needs comment. The matter contained here is very useful in providing in-service education to teachers.

Organisation of School Experiences

Part A lays emphasis on two important experiences i.e. free play time and participation in management and organisational work.

The document is silent on the operational part of these programmes—the crux of the problem.

One is at a loss to understand as to why a special mention is made of history along with social sciences. This creates the impression that history is not a part of social sciences.

4

Curricular Areas, School Stages and Assessment

The chapter 3 of the draft of National Curriculum Framework 2005 deals with the Curriculum Areas, School Stages and Assessment. It precedes the observations as under—

The main areas relevant for curricular planning have remained remarkably stable for a long time, despite major changes in social expectations and the academic study of different broad disciplines. It is important that each curricular area is revisited in depth, so that specific points of entry can be identified in the context of emerging social needs. In this respect, the status and role of the arts and physical education deserve special attention in view of the peculiar orbit of the 'extra-curricular' to which they were relegated almost a century ago. Aesthetic sensibility and experience being the prime sites of the growing child's creativity, we must bring the arts squarely into the domain of the curricular, infusing them in all areas of learning while giving them an identity of their own at relevant stages. Work, peace and health have a similar case. All three have a fundamental significance for economic, social and personal development. Schools have a major role to play in ensuring that children are socialised into a culture of self-reliance, resourcefulness, peace-oriented values and health.

3.1 LANGUAGE

Language provides a bank of memories and symbols inherited from one's fellow speakers and created in one's own life-time. It is also a medium through which most knowledge is constructed, and hence it is closely tied to the thoughts and identity of the individual. In fact, it is so closely bound with identity that to deny or wipe out a child's mother tongue(s) is to interfere with the sense of self. Effective understanding and use of languages(s) enables the child to make connections between ideas, people, and things and to relate to the world around.

Children are born with an innate language faculty. We know from our everyday experiences that most children, even before they start their schooling, have internalised an extremely complex and rule-governed system called language, and possess full linguistic capabilities. The teaching of language must begin by recognising this innate potential of the learner as a rich resource. Children with impairments who cannot use the standard spoken languages have also developed alternative sign and symbol systems for expression and communication. Language(s) in education would ideally build on this resource and would strive to enrich it through the development of literacy (scripts including Braille) for the acquisition of academic knowledge. Children with language-related impairments should be introduced to standard sign languages, which can support their continued growth and development to the fullest.

A recognition of the linguistic abilities of learners would encourage them to believe in themselves and their cultural moorings. Multilingualism which is constitutive of the identity of a child and a typical feature of the Indian linguistic landscape must be used as a resource by a creative language teacher. This is not only the best use of a resource readily available, but also a way of ensuring that every child feels secure and accepted, and no one is left behind on account of their linguistic background.

3.1.1 Language Education

The linguistic diversity of India poses complex challenges but also a range of opportunities. For the country as a whole, the large number of languages constitute a valuable cultural resource. India is unique not only in that a large number of languages are spoken here but also in terms of the number and variety of language families that are represented in those languages. There is no other country in the world in which languages from five different language families exist. Even though they are so distinct structurally as to merit classification as different language families, namely, Indo-Aryan, Dravidian, Austro-Asiatic, Tibeto-Burman and Andamanese-they constantly interact with each other. There are several linguistic and sociolinguistic features that are shared across languages which bear witness to the fact that different languages and cultures have co-existed in India for centuries enriching each other. Classical languages such as Latin, Arabic, Persian, Tamil and Sanskrit are rich in their inflectional grammatical structure and aesthetic value, and can illuminate our lives, as many language keep borrowing words from them.

Today, we know for certain that bilingualism or multilingualism confers definite cognitive advantages. Several studies have shown that bilingual proficiency raises the levels of cognitive growth, social tolerance, divergent thinking and scholastic achievement. Societal or national level multilingualism is a resource that can be favourably compared to any other national resource. The three-language formula is an attempt to address the challenges and opportunities of the linguistic situation in India. The following provisioning of language learning opportunities may help us achieve its aim:

- Mother tongue(s) of children should be the medium of instruction in schools.
- If regional language is not the learner's mother tongue, the first two years of education must still be covered through the mother tongue.
- At the primary level, children will study the state or regional language as a compulsory subject.
- In the middle school, children continue studying the state language(s) and also study English.
- In the non-Hindi states, children learn Hindi. In the case of Hindi states, children learn a language not spoken in their area. Sanskrit may also be studied as an MIL in addition to these languages.
- In the high school, a classical language may be introduced and in the higher secondary a foreign language may also be introduced.
- Language teaching needs to be multilingual not only in terms of the number of the languages offered to children but also in terms of evolving strategies that would use the multilingual classroom as a resource.

3.1.2 First Language Education

It is clear that through interaction with the family and other people around her, each child comes to acquire her language—or in many cases, languages. Thus children enter school with considerable communicative skills. Honing these skills by progressively fostering advanced level communicative and cognitive abilities in the classroom is the goal of first language education. From class III onwards, oracy and literacy will be tools for learning and for developing higher order communicative skills and critical thinking. At the primary stage the child's language must be accepted as it is, with no attempt to correct it. By Class IV the child should be made aware of the standard language and the rules of correct orthography, but care must be taken to honour and respect the child's home language(s). It should be accepted that errors are a necessary part of the process of learning and children will correct themselves *only* when they are ready to do so. Instead of focussing attention on errors and hard spots, it would be much better to spend time providing children comprehensible, interesting and challenging input.

Language education is not confined to the language classroom. A science, social science or mathematics class is, *ipso facto*, a language class. Learning the subject means learning the terminology, understanding the concepts, and being able to discuss and write about them critically. For some topics, students should be encouraged to consult books or talk to people in different languages, or gather material in English from the Internet. Such a policy of *languages across the curriculum* will foster a genuine multilingualism in the school. At the same time the language class offers some unique opportunities. Stories, poetry, songs and drama link children to their cultural heritage and also give them an opportunity to understand their own experiences and to develop sensitivity to others.

While many of the differently abled learners may pick up basic language skills through normal social interactions, they could additionally be provided with specially designed materials that would assist and enhance their growth and development. Studying sign language and Braille could be included as options for learners without disabilities.

3.1.3 Language is in Every Subject

Language—as a constellation of skills, thought encoders and markers of identity—cuts across school subjects and disciplines. Speech and listening, reading and writing are all generalised skills, and children's mastery over them becomes the key factor affecting success at school. In many situations, all of these skills need to be used together. This is why it is important to view language education as everybody's concern at school, and not as a responsibility of the language teacher alone. Also, the foundational role of the skills associated with language does not stop with the primary or elementary classes, but extends all the way up to the secondary and senior secondary classes as new needs arise in the subject areas.

The conventionally trained language teacher associates the training of speech with *correctness*, rather than with the expressive and participatory functions of language. This is why talking in class has a negative value in our system, and a great deal of the teacher's energy goes into keeping children quiet, or getting them to pronounce correctly. If teachers see the child's talk as a resource rather than as nuisance, the vicious cycle of resistance and control would have a chance to be turned into a cycle of expression and response. There is a vast body of knowledge available on how talk can be used as a resource and pre-and in-service teacher education programmes must introduce teachers to this. Designers of textbooks and teacher manuals could also plan and provide precise guidance to teachers regarding ways in which the subject matter can be explored further with the help of small-group talk among children, and undertaking activities that nurture the abilities to compare and contrast, to wonder and remember, to guess and challenge, to judge and evaluate.

In the orbit of listening, similar detailed planning of activities for incorporation in textbooks and teacher manuals would go a long way in resurrecting this significant skill and value area. It covers the ability to pay attention, to value the other person's point, to stay in touch with an unfolding utterance, and to make flexible hypotheses abut the meaning of what is being said. Listening, thus, forms as complex a web of skills and values as talking does. Locally available resources include folklore and storytelling, community singing and theatre. Storytelling is appropriate not only for pre-school education, but continues to be significant even later. As narrative discourse, an orally told story builds the foundations of logical understanding even as it enriches imagination and the capacity to participate vicariously in situations distant from one's life. Fantasy and mystery play an important role in child development. As a sector of language learning, listening also needs to be enriched with the help of music, which includes both folk, classical and popular composition. Folklore and music also deserve a place in language textbooks as discourses capable of being developed with the help of exercises and activities unique to them.

While **reading** is readily accepted as a focus area for language education, school syllabi are burdened with information and memorising tasks, so much so that the pleasure of reading for its own sake gets missed out. Opportunities for individualised reading need to be built at all stages in order to promote a reading culture, and teachers must set the example of being members of such a culture. This requires the nurturing of school and community libraries. The perception that reading of fiction is a waste of time acts as a major means of discouraging reading. Development and supply of a range of supplementary reading material relevant to all school subjects and across the grades requires urgent attention. A great deal of such material, though of varying quality, is available in the market, and could be utilised in a methodical manner to expand the scope of classroom teaching of a subject. Teacher training programmes need to familiarise teachers with such material and to give them yardsticks by which to select and use it effectively.

The importance of **writing** is well recognised, but the curriculum needs to attend to its innovative treatments. Teachers insist that children write in a *correct* way. Whether they express their own thoughts and feelings through writing is not considered too important. Just as the prematurely imposed discipline of pronunciation stifles the child's motivation to talk freely, in his or her own dialect, for instance, the demand for writing in mechanically correct ways blocks the urge to use writing to express or to convey one's ideas. Teachers need to be persuaded and trained to place writing in the same domain as artistic expression, and to cease perceiving it as an office skill. During the primary years, writing abilities should be developed holistically in conjunction with the sensibilities associated with talking, listening, and reading. At middle and senior levels of schooling, note-making should receive attention as a skilldevelopment training. This will go a long way in discouraging mechanical copying from the blackboard, textbooks and guides. Effort is also necessary to break the routinisation of tasks like letter and essay writing, so that allow for imagination and originality play a more prominent role in education.

Reading Pedagogy

The failure of many children to learn to read and write even after three or more years of schooling is cause for concern. This is one of the most significant school related reasons why children drop out. There are many reasons, some of them beyond the purview of the classroom. However, what happens—or fails to happen—in the classroom is also a contributing factor. In India there has been little research, debate or experimentation on the methods of teaching beginning reading. It has generally not been recognised that for most Indian languages, unlike English, there is a one-to-one relationship between character and sound. This means that the task of learning to read an Indian language should be considerably easier than learning to read English (although this advantage is offset somewhat by the greater visual complexity of the Indian scripts).

In response to the perceived failure of our schools in the teaching of reading, some institutions have uncritically adopted a single methodology and undertaken cascade models of mass training. This should be reconsidered. Even in a single classroom no one method is adequate. Ultimately an eclectic approach employing a number of complementary methods may have to be adopted.

3.1.4 Second Language Teaching

The goals, method and content of second language teaching will vary according to the degree of students' familiarity with the language and their attitude towards it. Care must be taken in the selection of texts ensuring that they engage children and demonstrate the vibrancy and relevance of the living language, and retain their interest rather than act as mere carriers of culture and morality.

3.1.5 English

The teaching of English is a central language curriculum question for all schools in the country. On the one hand the failure of a large number of children in class X examination on account of English is a patently unfair judgment of children. On the other hand is the increasing pressure to include the teaching of English as a subject from class I, if not English as the medium of instruction. If we compel children to give up their own language early in their life and fill that space with only, say, English, we make them incapable of relating to the Indian surroundings as the words at their disposal are only the English ones. But it is necessary to address the question of developing effective competence in a language that is now an essential part of aspirations and access to opportunities of livelihood, knowledge and power.

English education would be meaningful only when it succeeds in finding its place along with other Indian languages. Parallel texts in more than one language, bilingual dictionaries for higher classes, talking books and Big Books would help change schools into a print rich environment. Posting the school with signs, charts, notices and labels, and other semiotic structures would help teachers make the learning environment more experiential. The texts should have stories, poems, and other writings which relate to the culture that the learner comes from. Now that there is a lot of writing in English, and textbook designers should turn to them in place of archaic texts that have been in use for nearly a century in some parts of the country. The texts should also reflect the multicultural diversity and variety that obtains in the classroom.

3.2 MATHEMATICS

Developing children's abilities for mathematisation is the main goal of mathematics education. The narrow aim of school mathematics is to develop 'useful' capabilities, particularly those relating to numeracy—numbers, number operations, measurement, decimals and percentages. The higher aim is to develop the child's resources to think and reason mathematically, to pursue assumptions to logical conclusions and to handle abstraction. It includes a way of doing things, and the ability and the attitude, to formulate and solve problems.

This calls for a curriculum that is ambitious, coherent and teaches important mathematics. It should be ambitious in the sense that it seeks to achieve the higher aim mentioned above rather than only the narrower aim. It should be coherent in the sense that the variety of methods and skills available piecemeal (in arithmetic, algebra, geometry) cohere into an ability to address problems that come from other domains such as science and social studies in high school. It should be important in the sense that students feel the need to solve such problems, that teachers and students find it worth their time and energy to address these problems. The twin concerns of the mathematics curriculum are: what can mathematics education do to engage the mind of every student, and how can it strengthen the student's resources?

As mathematics is a compulsory subject the secondary stage, access to quality mathematics education is the right of every child. In the context of univeralisation of education, the first question to ask is, what mathematics can be offered in eight years of schooling that will stand every child in good stead rather than be a preparation for higher secondary education alone. Most of the skills taught in primary school mathematics are useful. However, a reorientation of curriculum towards addressing the 'higher aims' mentioned above will make better use of the time children spend in school in terms of problem solving and analytical skills it builds, and prepare children better to meet a wide variety of problems in life. Also instead of a 'tall and narrow' curriculum, one that has more topics that are closer to the ground and that are more broad based, would serve the needs of different learners better.

3.2.1 Vision for School Mathematics

- Children learn to enjoy mathematics rather than fear it.
- Children learn important mathematics: Mathematics is more than formulas and mechanical procedures.
- Children see mathematics as something to talk about, to communicate, to discuss among themselves, to work together on.
- Children pose and solve meaningful problems.
- Children use abstractions to perceive relationships, to see structure, to reason out things, to argue the truth or falsity of statements.
- Children understand the basic structure of mathematics: Arithmetic, algebra, geometry and trigonometry, the basic content areas of school mathematics, all offer a methodology for abstraction, structuration and generalisation.
- Teachers engage every child in class with the conviction that everyone can learn mathematics.

Many general **tactics of problem solving** can be taught,

progressively during the stages of school: abstraction, quantification, analogy, case analysis, reduction to simpler situations, even guessand-verify, are useful in many problem contexts. Moreover, when children learn a variety of approaches (over time), their toolkit gets richer and they also learn which approach is best when. Children also need exposure to the use of heuristics, or rules of thumb, rather than only believe that mathematics is an 'exact science'. The **estimation of quantities and approximating solutions** is also an absolutely essential skill. When a farmer estimates the yield of a particular crop, considerable skills in **estimation, approximation and optimisation** are used. School mathematics can play a significant role in developing and honing such useful skills.

Visualisation and **representation** are skills that mathematics can help to develop. **Modelling** situations using quantities, shapes and forms is the best use of mathematics. Mathematical concepts can be represented in multiple ways and representations can serve a variety of purposes in different contexts – all of this adds to the power of mathematics. For example, a function may be represented in algebraic form or in the form of a graph. The representation p/q can be used to denote a fraction as a part of the whole, but can also denote the quotient of two numbers p and q. Learning this about fractions is as important, if not more so, than learning the arithmetic of fractions. There is also need to make **connections** between mathematics and other subjects of study. When children learn to draw graphs, they should also be encouraged to think of functional relationships in the sciences, including geology. Our children need to appreciate the fact that mathematics is an effective instrument in science.

The importance of systematic reasoning in mathematics cannot be overemphasised, and is intimately tied to notions of **aesthetics** and **elegance** dear to mathematicians. Proof is important, but in addition to deductive proof, children should also learn when pictures and constructions provide proof. Proof is a process that convinces a skeptical adversary; school mathematics should encourage proof as a systematic way of argumentation. The aim should be to develop arguments, evaluate arguments, make and investigate conjectures, and understand that there are various methods of reasoning.

Mathematical communication, which is precise and with unambiguous use of language and rigour in formulation are important characteristics of mathematical treatment. The use of jargon in mathematics is deliberate, conscious and stylised. Mathematicians discuss what is appropriate notation since good notation is held and thought as to aid thought. As children grow older, they should be taught to appreciate the significance of such conventions and their use. For instance, this means that setting up of equations should get as much coverage as solving them.

In discussing many of these skills and processes, we have referred to a **multiplicity of approaches** and **procedures**. These are all crucial for liberating school mathematics from the tyranny of applying the only those algorithms that are taught.

3.2.2 The Curriculum

At the **pre-primary stage**, all learning occurs through play rather than through didactic communication. Rather than the rote learning of the number sequence, children need to learn and understand, in the context of small sets, the connection between word names and counting, and between counting and quantity. Making simple comparisons and classifications, along one dimension at a time, and identifying shapes and symmetry are appropriate skills to acquire at this stage. Encouraging children to use language to freely express one's thoughts and emotions, rather than in pre-determined ways is extremely important at this and at later stages.

Having children develop a positive attitude towards and a liking for mathematics at the **primary stage** is as important, if not more so, than the cognitive skills and concepts that they acquire. Mathematical games, puzzles and stories help in developing a positive attitude and in making connections between mathematics and everyday thinking. It is important to note that mathematics is not just arithmetic. Besides numbers and number operations, due place must be given to shapes, spatial understanding, patterns, measurement and data handling. The curriculum must explicitly incorporate the progression that learners make from the concrete to the abstract while accquring concepts. Apart from computational skills, stress must be laid on identifying, expressing and explaining patterns, on estimation and approximation in solving problems, on making connections and on the development of skills of language in communication and reasoning.

At the **upper primary stage,** students obtain a first taste of the power of mathematics through the application of powerful abstract concepts that compress previous learning and experience. This enables them to revisit and consolidate basic concepts and skills learnt at primary school, which is essential from the point of view of achieving universal mathematical literacy. Students are introduced to algebraic notation and its use in solving problems and in generalisation, to the systematic study of space and shapes, and consolidate their knowledge of measurement.

Data handling, representation and interpretation form a significant part of the ability to deal with information in general, which is an essential 'life skill'. The learning at this stage also offers an opportunity to enrich students' spatial reasoning and visualisation skill.

At the **secondary stage**, the student begins to perceive the structure of mathematics as a discipline. She becomes familiar with the characteristics of mathematical communication: carefully defined terms and concepts, the use of symbols to represent them, precisely stated propositions, and proofs justifying propositions. These aspects are developed particularly in the area of geometry. Students develop their facility with algebra, which is important not only in the application of mathematics, but also within mathematics in providing justifications and proofs. At this stage the student integrates the many concepts and skill she has learnt into a problem solving ability. Mathematical modelling, data analysis and interpretation taught at this stage can consolidate a high level of mathematical literacy. Individual and group exploration of connections and patterns, visualisation and generalisation, making and proving conjectures is important at this stage and can be encouraged through the use of appropriate tools such as computers and concrete models and aids.

The aim of the mathematics curriculum at the **higher secondary stage** is to provide the student with an appreciation of the wide variety of the application of mathematics, and with the basic tools that enable such application. A careful choice between the often conflicting demands of depth versus breadth needs to be made at this stage. The rapid explosion of mathematics as a discipline and of its range of application favours an increase in the breadth of coverage. Such increase must be dictated by mathematical considerations of the importance of topics to be included. Topics that are more naturally the province of other disciplines may be left out of the mathematics curriculum. The treatment of topics must have as an objective, the communication of mathematical insight and concepts, which naturally arouse the interest and engagement of students.

3.2.3 Computer Science and Mathematics

The tremendous effectiveness of the computer and computing technology in shaping modern society has created the need for an educated public that can utilise such technology most effectively for the betterment of society and humankind. There is therefore a growing realisation of the need to have place for these domains of knowledge in the school curriculum.

A distinction must be made between the IT (Information Technology) curriculum which involves the use and applications of tools of the information and computer age and the CS (Computer Science) curriculum, which is concerned with how these tools are designed and deployed. Both of these have their place in school education.

While several countries have implemented CS and/or IT curricula in schools, we need to be aware of the challenges that Indian school students face. The first of these is the paucity of technology resources for computer science. It is absurd to teach computer science (let alone computer usage) without access to computing resources. Providing computer access and connectivity for all children is a tremendous technological and economic challenge. However, given the pervasive impact of computer technologies, we need to seriously address this infrastructure challenge and explore viable and innovative alternatives with regard to hardware, software and connectivity technologies appropriate for rural and urban Indian schools.

We also need to address the issue of the development of a comprehensive and coherent curriculum model in computer science and information technology, which can serve as the basis for the beginning of a discussion between educators, administrators, and the general public. Certain core elements are common to several CS and IT curricula and are applicable to Indian schools as well. These include the concepts of iterative processes and algorithms, general problem solving strategies arising from computing, possibilities of computer usage, the place occupied by computers in the modern world and the societal issues that arise thereby.

3.3 NATURAL SCIENCES

The inquiring and imaginative human mind has responded to the wonder and awe of nature in different ways. Observing the physical and biological environment carefully, looking for any meaningful patterns and relations, making and using new tools to interact with nature, and build conceptual models to understand the world has led to modern science.

Science is a dynamic, expanding body of knowledge covering ever new domains of experience. As with many complex things in life, the scientific method is perhaps more easily discerned than defined. But broadly speaking, it involves several interconnected steps: observation, looking for regularities and patterns, making hypotheses, devising qualitative or mathematical models, deducing their consequences; verification or falsification of theories through observations and controlled experiments, and thus arriving at the principles, theories and laws governing the physical world. There is no strict order in these various steps. Sometimes, a theory may suggest a new experiment; at other times an experiment may suggest a new theoretical model. Speculation and conjecture also have a place in science, but ultimately, a scientific theory, to be acceptable, must be verified by relevant observations and/or experiments. The laws of science are never viewed as fixed eternal truths. Even the most established and universal laws of science are always regarded as provisional, subject to modification in the light of new observations, experiments and analysis.

Good science education is true to the child, true to life and true to science. This simple observation leads to the following basic criteria of validity of a science curriculum:

1. *Cognitive validity* requires that the content, process, language and pedagogical practices of the curriculum are age appropriate, and within the cognitive reach of the child.
2. *Content validity* requires that the curriculum must convey significant and correct scientific content. Simplification of content, which is necessary to adapt the curriculum to the cognitive level of the learner, must not be so trivialised as to convey something basically flawed and/or meaningless.
3. *Process validity* requires that the curriculum engage the learner in acquiring the methods and processes that lead to generation and validation of scientific knowledge, and nurture the natural curiosity and creativity of the child in science. Process validity is an important criterion since it helps the student in 'learning to learn' science.
4. *Historical validity* requires that science curriculum be informed by a historical perspective, enabling the learner to appreciate how the concepts of science evolve with time. It also helps the learner to view science as a social enterprise and to understand how social factors influence the development of science.
5. *Environmental validity* requires that science be placed in the wider context of the learner's environment, local and global, enabling him/her to appreciate the issues at the interface of science, technology and society and preparing him/her with the requisite knowledge and skills to enter the world of work.
6. *Ethical validity* requires that the curriculum promote the values of honesty, objectivity, cooperation, freedom from fear and prejudice, and develop in the learner a concern for life and preservation of environment.

3.3.1 The Curriculum at Different Stages

Consistent with the criteria above, the objectives, content, pedagogy and assessment for different stages of the curriculum are as follows:

At the Primary stage the child should be engaged in joyfully exploring the world around and harmonising with it. The objectives at this stage are to nurture the curiosity of the child about the world (natural environment, artifacts and people), to have the child engage in exploratory and hands on activities to acquire the basic cognitive and psychomotor skills through observation, classification, inference, etc.; to emphasise design and fabrication, estimation and measurement as a prelude to development of technological and quantitative skills of later stages; and to develop the basic language skills: speaking, reading and writing not only for science but also through science. Science and social science should be integrated as '*Environmental Studies*' as at present, with health as an important component. Throughout the primary stage, there should be no formal periodic tests, no awarding of grades or marks, and no detention.

At the Upper Primary stage the child should be engaged in learning principles of science through familiar experiences, working with hands to design simple technological units and modules and continuing to learn more about environment and health through activities and surveys. Scientific concepts are to be arrived at mainly from activities and experiments. Science content at this stage is not to be regarded as a diluted version of secondary school science. Group activity, discussions with peers and teachers, surveys, organisation of data and their display through exhibitions, etc. in schools and neighbourhood are to be an important component of pedagogy. There should be continuous as well as periodic assessment (unit tests, term end tests). The system of 'direct' grades should be adopted. There should be no detention. Every child who attends eight years of school should be eligible to enter Class IX.

At the Secondary stage the students should be engaged in learning science as a composite discipline, in working with hands and tools to design more advanced technological modules than at the upper primary stage, and in activities and analysis on issues surrounding environment and health. Systematic experimentation as a tool to discover/verify theoretical principles, and the Scientific and Technological Literacy (STL) model of working on locally significant projects are to be important parts of the curriculum at this stage.

At the Higher Secondary stage science should be introduced as separate disciplines with emphasis on experiments/technology and problem solving. The current two streams, academic and vocational, being pursued as per NPE 1986 may require a relook in the present scenario. The students may be given an option to choose the subjects of their interest freely, though it may not be feasible to offer all the different subjects in every school. The curriculum load should be rationalised to avoid the steep gradient between secondary and higher secondary syllabus, but care should be taken not to compromise the present internationally comparable standards of our syllabus.

3.3.2 Outlook

Looking at the complex scenario of science education in India, three issues stand out. First, science education is still far from achieving the goal of equity enshrined in our Constitution. Second, science education in India, even at its best, develops competence but does not encourage inventiveness and creativity. Third, the overpowering examination system is basic to most, if not all, the fundamental problems of science education in India.

The science curriculum must be used as an instrument of social change to reduce the divide related to economic class, gender, caste, religion and region. We must use textbooks as one of the primary instruments for equity, since for a great majority of school going children, as also for their teachers, it is the only accessible and affordable resource for education. We must encourage alternative textbook writing in the country within the broad guidelines of the national curriculum framework. These textbooks should incorporate activities, observation and experimentation, and enhance an active approach to science, connecting it with the world around the child, rather than infortion based learning. Added to this materials such as workbooks, supplementary reading, and children's encyclopaedia would enhance children's access to information and ideas that need not go into the textbook, loading it, but would enrich learning that takes place through project work. There is a dearth of such materials with rich visuals in regional languages.

The development of science corners, and providing access to science experimentation kits and laboratories in rural areas are also important facets of equitable provisioning for science learning. Information and Communication Technology (ICT) is an important tool for bridging the social divides. ICT should be used in such a way that it becomes an opportunity equalizer, by providing information, communication and computing resources in remote areas. ICT if used to connect children and teachers with scientists working in universities and research institutions would also help to demystify scientists and their work.

For any qualitative change from the present situation, science education in India must undergo a paradigm shift. Rote learning should be discouraged. Inquiry skills should be supported and strengthened by language, design and quantitative skills. Schools should give much greater emphasis on co-curricular and extra curricular elements aimed at stimulating investigative ability, inventiveness and creativity, even if these elements are not part of the external examination system. An ongoing movement along the lines of the Children's Science Congress held with great success at present. Gradually, such a movement should spread to the every corner of India and enter across South Asia, creating a wave of creativity and scientific temper among the young and their teachers.

Examination reform, supported by funding and high quality human resources and bringing teachers, educationists and scientists on a common platform, should launch new ways of testing students which would reduce the high level of examination related stress, curb the maddening multiplicity of entrance examinations, and research on ways of testing multiple abilities other than formal scholastic competence.

These reforms, however, fundamentally need the over-arching reform of teacher empowerment. No reform, however well motivated and well planned, can succeed unless a majority of teachers feel empowered to put it in practice. With active teacher participation, the reforms suggested above could have a cascading effect on all stages of science teaching in our schools.

3.4 SOCIAL SCIENCES

The social sciences encompass diverse concerns of society and include a wide a range of content, drawn from the disciplines of history, geography, political science, economics and sociology. The selection and organisation of material into a meaningful social science curriculum, enabling students to develop a critical understanding of society, is therefore a challenging task. The possibilities of including new dimensions and concerns are immense, especially in view of the student's own life experiences.

It is important to reinstate the significance of the social sciences by not only highlighting its increasing relevance for work opportunities in the expanding service sector, but also by pointing to its indispensability in laying the foundations for an analytical and creative mindset. The tendency to treat the social sciences as being less important or challenging than the natural science or mathematics needs to be questioned.

The social sciences carry a normative responsibility to create and widen the popular base for peace-oriented human values, such as freedom, justice and respect for diversity. Social science teaching should be aimed at investing in a child children moral and mental energy so as to provide them with the ability to think independently and deal with the social forces that threaten these values, without losing her individuality. Social Science teaching can achieve this by promoting children's ability to take initiative to critically reflect on social issues that have a bearing on creative coexistence between individual good and collective good. Critical reflection pre-supposes a comprehensive curriculum in which learners – both teachers and children – participate in generating knowledge without any latent and manifest forces of coercion. It is through this non-coercive and participatory mode that children and teachers stand the best chance of making teaching and learning interesting and enjoyable.

The disciplines that make up the social sciences, namely history, geography, political science and economics, have distinct methodologies that often justify the preservation of boundaries. At the same time, the boundaries of these disciplines need to be opened up and a plurality of approaches may be applied to understand a given phenomenon. For an enabling curriculum, the inclusion of themes that facilitate interdisciplinary thinking are required.

3.4.1 The Proposed Epistemological Frame

Based on certain considerations of dominant perceptions as well as issues to be addressed the following points serve as the foundational logic in the drafting of new syllabi:

- The curriculum must be able to show, how the nation and national unity figures in local perceptions of the people. Local perceptions, therefore, have to be articulated through reorienting curriculum
- The notion of textbook be changed from being merely instructive to more suggestive. It is argued that this would offer enough scope for the learner even to go beyond the very textbook, creating more appetite for further reading that is necessary to enrich the understanding of a given social phenomenon.
- The major thrust of the social science curriculum has remained utilitarian in nature. That is to say, it puts more emphasis on developmental issues that are important but does not sufficient by help to understand the normative dimension – issues of equality, justice the and dignity of society and polity. Teaching of social science, has thus been linked up to the role of an individual in contributing to this 'development'. In view of this gap, there is a need to achieve a shift in focus from utilitarianism to egalitarianism that would address the normative concerns mentioned above.
- It is suggested to bring a change in nomenclature from civics to political science. Civics as a subject had appeared in the Indian school curriculum in the colonial period in the background of

increasing 'disloyalty' among Indians towards the Raj. Emphasis on the obedience and loyalty of the citizens and creation of civil society according to the universal values of progress were the key features of colonial civics. Now that democracy in India has matured to the point where power is being evolved to be given opportunity to study political structures and values necessary for the further evolution of participatory democracy. Especially in the context of values like equality and justice, schools need to encourage children and teachers to analyse issues relevant for dealing with marginalisation and oppression. Whereas political science offers a dynamic means of studying contemporary society and therefore a pedagogical sphere where more informed, receptive and responsible citizens could be produced.

- Gender concerns need to be addressed in terms of making the perspectives of women integral to the discussion of any historical event and contemporary concern. This shift from highlighting individuals to forefronting women's struggles both historically as well as on a daily basis, requires an epistemic shift from the patriarchal nationalist frame.

The concept of human rights has a universalistic frame of reference. Children need to be introduced to this wider orbit of values when they are young, in a manner appropriate for their age-specific psychology and terms. Human rights are a relevant concept for the organisation of knowledge in both social and natural sciences. Many everyday issues, such as water, work and other material designed for young readers so that they develop a spontaneous respect for human dignity and rights.

Human rights education is an imperative for achieving the aims of education, some components of which have been brought into the National Curriculum Framework and the content of various subjects. The National Curriculum Frameworks of 1975 and 1988 laid stress on some of the objectives, which are important for the programmes of human rights education in the school curriculum. The National Policy on Education (1986) defines the basic components of core curriculum all of which imply that importance should be given to concept of human rights for all stages of education. Values and ideas consistent with the concept of human rights enshrined in the Indian Constitution and its preamble such as social cohesion, secularism, national integration, socialism, fundamental rights, fundamental duties, directive principles of state policy and environment should be provided appropriate space in the school subjects, especially in social sciences. Human rights and Fundamental freedoms as defined in the United Nations Charter and the Universal Declaration of Human Rights need to permeate the entire content and process of education across subject areas.

3.4.2 Planning the Curriculum

At the early **primary stage**, the natural and social environment should be taught as an integral part of language and mathematics (with gender sensitivity). Children should be engaged in activities that would help them in promoting an understanding about the natural and social environment. Understanding at this level should be based on observation and illustration rather than abstractions. Illustrations need to be drawn from the physical, biological, social and cultural aspects of life. It is important for the child to develop the skill of observation, identification and classification.

For classes III to V, the subject environment studies should be used to train children to locate and comprehend the relationships between the natural and social environment. They should be introduced to analogies between natural diversity and socio-cultural diversity. That is to say, social science teaching based on observation and experience can create cognitive capacity and resourcefulness enabling the child to feel curious about social phenomena, starting with the family and moving on to wider spheres.

At the **upper primary stage**, the subject-area of social science drawing its content from history, geography, political science and economics could be introduced. Simultaneously, the child may be introduced to contemporary issues and problems which are looked at from multiple perspectives introducing the child to social and economic problems of society. Emphasis needs to be given to issues like poverty, illiteracy, child and bonded labour, class, caste, gender, the environment and human rights. Geography and economics may together help in developing a proper perspective related to the issues concerning environment and resources, and development at different levels. The child will be introduced to the formation and functioning of governments at the local, state and central level and the democratic processes of participation.

Given the importance of history in shaping consciousness of the past and the nuances of the child's growing identity as a citizen, it is essential that the approach to History, from the upper primary stage onwards, provides children with a sense of the historical past and a sense of wonder about its relics. For this the curriculum must overcome its conventional approach characterized by the treatment of regions by referring to their present-day political boundaries, rigid periodisation and indifference to children's cognitive development and capacity. Inclusion of archeology, visits to important local historical sites and museums, and the use of historical evidence on an illustrative basis could form key components of reforms in the teaching of history.

At the **secondary stage**, Social Sciences can comprise distinct elements of history, geography, political science and economics, with adequate space being offered to certain themes where the insights available in these distinct spheres can merge. The main focus should be on contemporary India and the learner will be initiated into a deeper understanding of the social and economic challenges facing the nation. In keeping with the epistemic shift proposed, contemporary India should be discussed from the perspectives of the adivasi, dalit and other marginalised populations. The effort should be to relate the content as much as possible to the children's everyday lives.

India's freedom struggle and the contributions of various sections and regions shall be studied. India's national movement and its development as an independent nation will be taught in the context of changes in the modern world.

Issues relating to geography should be taught keeping in mind the need to inculcate in the child a critical appreciation for conservation and environmental concerns. In political science the focus should be on discussing the philosophical foundations that underlie the value framework of the Indian Constitution, *i.e.* an in-depth discussion of equality, liberty, justice, fraternity, dignity, plurality and freedom from exploitation. As the disciplinary area of economics is being introduced to the child at this level, it is important that the topics discussed are chosen from the perspective of the masses. For example, poverty and unemployment may be derived from an understanding of the functioning of economic institutions and the inequalities entertained in economic relations.

The **higher secondary stage** is considered important as it offers diverse choice of streams to the students according to their need, interest and aptitude. For some of the students, this stage may be the end of their formal education leading to the world of work; for others, it provides a foundation for higher education. They may choose either specialized academic courses or job oriented vocational courses. The foundation laid at this stage should be able to equip them with basic knowledge, skills and attitudes towards making meaningful contributions in any field they choose.

A variety of courses from social sciences and commerce may be offered to students and they may exercise their choice, keeping in view their inclinations and preferences. Subjects and courses need not be grouped into separate streams but students may be given the choice of subjects or courses from any group according to their needs, interests and aptitude. At this stage, social sciences may include disciplines like political science, geography, history, archeology, economics, sociology and psychology. At the higher secondary stage, it is expected that the study of these subjects will enable children to develop the skills and abilities to make judgment, analyse rival claims and evidence, enter into debates, and undertake independent project work using a wide range of resources.

3.4.3 Approaches to Pedagogy and Resources

Social science teaching needs to be revitalised towards helping the learner acquire knowledge and skills in an interactive environment. The teaching of social sciences must adopt methods that promote creativity, aesthetics, and critical perspectives, and enable children to draw relationships between past and present, to understand changes taking place in society. Problem solving, dramatization and role play are some hitherto under-explored strategies that could be employed. Teaching should utilise greater resources of audio-visual materials, including photographs, charts and maps, and replicas of archaeological and material cultures.

In order to make the process of learning participative there is a need to shift from mere imparting of information to debate and discussion. This approach to learning will keep both the learner and teacher alive to social realities.

Concepts should be clarified to the students through the lived experiences of individuals and communities. It has often been observed that cultural, social and class differences generate their own biases, prejudices and attitudes in classroom contexts. The approach to teaching therefore needs to be open-ended. Teachers should discuss different dimensions of social reality in the class, and work towards creating increasing self-awareness amongst themselves and in the learners.

WATER AND THE ENVIRONMENT	
Were does water come from?	NATURAL SOURCES OF WATER
How are seas, oceans, rivers formed?	Rivers, lakes, seas Underground water
What are our local water resources?	WATER RESOURCE MAPPING Local/regional/national
Why do wells dry up? How do handpumps work?	Relationship Between Natural and Man-Made Sources of Water
Are big dams more beneficial than small dams?	Understanding the water table Handpumps Systems of irrigation Environmental impact of big dams

How do people in desert areas procure water?	WATER IN DIFFERENT Eco-Systems Water sources in desert areas Water sources in mountainous regions
What causes droughts?	Droughts and floods
SOCIAL ASPECTS OF WATER	
Who controls the village well?	CASTE AND CLASS Purity and pollution Control over water resources
Who fetches water?	GENDER DIVISION OF LABOUR AND WATER AVAILABILITY OF WATER
Do we have enough water?	Local and regional conflicts over drinking and irrigation water: Water as market forces
Why is clean water essential?	HEALTH Body's need for water Right to potable clean water Water borne diseases

3.5 ART EDUCATION

For decades now, the importance of arts in the education system has been repeatedly debated, discussed and recommended, without much progress in this direction. The need to integrate art education in the formal schooling of our students now requires urgent attention if we are to retain our unique cultural identity in all its diversity and richness. Far from encouraging the pursuit of arts, our education system has steadily discouraged young students and creative minds from taking to the arts or at best, permits them to consider the arts to be 'useful hobbies' and 'leisure activities'. Arts are reduced to tools for enhancing the prestige of the school on occasions like Independence Day, Founder's Day, Annual Day or during an inspection of the school's progress and working. Before or after that, the arts are abandoned for the better part of a child's school life and the student is herded towards subjects that are perceived as being more worthy of attention. General awareness of the arts is also ebbing steadily among not just students, but their guardians, teachers and even among policy makers and educationalists.

Schools and school authorities encourage arts of a superficial and popular nature and take pride in putting up events that showcase songs and dances and plays that may entertain, but have little aesthetic quality. We can no longer afford to ignore the importance of the arts and must concentrate all possible energies and resources towards nurturing artistic capabilities and creating cultural and artistic awareness amongst the students of vast and varied cultural inheritance we have. Arts in India are living examples of its secular fabric and cultural diversity. They include a variety of folk and classical forms of music and dance, theatre, puppetry, clay work, and visual arts, and crafts which cover every region of India. Learning any of these arts would enrich the lives of our young citizens, not only in their school years, but throughout their lives.

Arts, visual and performing, need to become an important component of learning in the curriculum. Children must develop skills and abilites in these areas, not as a mere entertaining fringe. Through the arts curriculum students must be introduced to the rich and varied artistic traditions in the country. Arts education must become both a tool and a subject taught in every school as a compulsory subject (up to class X) and facilities for the same may be provided in every school. All four main streams covered by the term arts, *i.e.* music, dance, visual arts and theatre, should be included. Awareness also needs to be built among parents and guardians, school authorities and administrators regarding the importance of arts. Emphasis should be given on learning than teaching, and the approach should be participatory, interactive, and experiential rather than instructive.

Through out the years of school, in all stages, the medium and forms of art allow children to develop both a playful as well as a disciplined exploration of themselves and materials, and allows them with many ways of expression. Music, dance and theatre all contribute to the development of self, both cognitive and social. The importance of such experiences in the pre-primary and primary school years cannot be over-emphasised.

Language, exploration of nature and deepening understanding of self and others can all be experientially learnt and understood by children through art forms. By their nature, the art forms also allow very differentially-abled children to participate alongside each other, without differences being significant.

Resources for the integration of arts and heritage crafts should be available in every school. Thus, it is important that the curriculum provide adequate time for a range of art activities. Block periods of about one hour to one-and-half hour are necessary especially where theatre or dance, clay-work are involved. The emphasis should not be on attaining some adult standards or notions of 'perfect art', but on supporting the child's own expression and style through exposure to material, skills and technique, but without over-emphasis on them. Over the years teachers would help children to move towards independently formulating and executing their own art projects with dedication and persistence, a sense of aesthetic quality and of excellence.

In the secondary and higher secondary school stages, the art curriculum may allow children to specialize in some areas of their interest. Along with learning the skills and practicing them, children could also at this stage learn some of the theory related to art and aesthetic experience, which could deepen their appreciation and also help them understand the significance of this area of knowledge. Discussions on popular cultural art forms, different kinds of art-traditions (cultural differences) and creativity, would also provide them with a perspective on the variety of forms and 'taste'. It is important therefore that the curriculum not be biased and judgemental about high or low forms of culture, nor treat classical and folk art forms differently. It would also prepare those who wish to choose an art form for specialized study in their +2 stage, or even consider pursuing a career in arts.

More resource material on arts education should be made available for arts education teachers. Teacher education and orientation must include a significant component that will enable teachers to efficiently and creatively include arts education. In addition, Bal-Bhavans which have played an important role in the urban scape should proliferate and be established at district headquarters, and eventually at all

3.6 HEALTH AND PHYSICAL EDUCATION

It is well acknowledged that health is a multidimensional concept and is shaped by biological, social, economic, cultural and political factors. Access to basic needs like food, safe water supply, housing, sanitation and health services influences the health status of a population and these are reflected through mortality and nutritional indicators. Health is a critical input for the overall development of the child and it influences significantly enrolment, retention and completion of school. This curriculum area adopts a holistic definition of health within which physical education and yoga contribute to the physical, social, emotional and mental development of a child.

Under-nutrition and communicable diseases are the major health problems faced by majority of the children in this country, from pre-primary through to the higher secondary school stage. Therefore the need to address this aspect at all levels of schooling with special attention to vulnerable social groups and girl children. It is proposed that the mid-day meal programme and medical check ups be made a part of the curriculum and education about health be provided which address the age specific concerns at different stages of development. The idea of a comprehensive school health programme, conceived in the 1940's, included six major components viz. medical care, hygienic school environment, and school lunch, health and physical education. These components are important for the overall development of the child and hence need to be included as a part of the curriculum. The more recent addition to the curriculum is yoga. The entire group must be taken together as a comprehensive health and physical education curriculum, rather than the fragmentary approach current in schools today. As a core part of the curriculum, time allocated for games and for yoga must not be cut down, or taken away under any circumstances.

Given the interdisciplinary nature of health, there are many opportunities for cross curricular learning and integration. Activities such as the National Service Scheme, Bharat Scouts and Guides and the National Cadet Corps, are some such areas. The sciences provide opportunities to learn about physiology, health and disease, and the interdependencies between various living organisms, and the physical habitat. Social sciences could provide insights into community health as well as understanding the spread, control and cure of infectious diseases, as well as from a socio-economic and global perspective. This subject lends itself for applied learning and innovative approaches can be adopted for transacting the curriculum.

The importance of this subject to the overall development needs to be reinforced at the policy level, with administrators, other subject teachers in schools, the health department, parents and children. Recognising health and physical education and core and compulsory, ensuring the material equipment and sports and yoga instructors are available, and that doctors and medical personel visit school regularly, are some of the steps that can be taken. Further, this subject could be offered as an elective at the plus two level.

The 'needs based approach' could guide the dimensions of physical, psycho-social and mental aspects that need to be included at different levels of schooling. A basic understanding of the concerns is necessary, but the more important dimension is that of experience and development of health, skills and physique through practical engagements with play, exercises, sports, and practices of personal and community hygiene. Collective and individual responsibilities for health and community living need to be emphasised. Several national health programmes like the Reproductive and Child Health, HIV/AIDs, Tuberculosis and Mental Health have been targeting children as a focus group for with prevention in view. These demands on children need to be integrated into exisiting curricular activities rather than adding on.

Yoga could be introduced from the primary level onwards in informal ways, but formal introduction of *asanas* and *dhyana* should begin only from class sixth onwards. Even health and hygiene education must rely on the practical and experiential dimensions of children's lives. There can be more emphasis on the inclusion of sports and games from the local area. Learning games played in different parts of country and world.

It should be possible to organize the utilization of the school space at the block level at least, for a special sports programme both before school hours and after school hours to enable children with special talents for sports to come here for special training, and during vacation periods. It should also be possible to develop these sports facilties so that many more children come here for leisure time sports activities and engage with team games such as basket ball, throw ball, volley ball, and local forms of sports.

3.7 WORK AND EDUCATION

Work, understood simply, is an activity that involves labour. It is making or doing something that is valued by society. It also means making one's labour or capabilities, or both, available for someone else's purposes for monetary returns. A number of these activities are related to producing food, articles of daily use and looking after physical and mental well-being of people. Other activities relate to administration and organisation in society. In any society, in addition to these two basic dimensions, (producing goods and establishing smooth functioning) various other forms of activity also contribute to human wellbeing, and in that sense become forms of work. This includes inventing, sport and performing arts.

Understood in this sense, work implies **commitment to other members** of the society/community as one is contributing one's labour and capabilities to fulfil their needs. Second, it implies **submitting to public standards of performance** as one's contribution made through work will be valued and judged by others. Third, work implies **contribution to the functioning of social life** as it either produces something that makes life possible or helps in functioning in general. Finally, work **enriches human life** as it opens up new dimensions of appreciation and enjoyment.

Thus an experience of involvement in productive work in an educational setting should make one appreciate the worth of social life and what is valued and appreciated in society. Work also brings relations to a more concrete level by adding cooperation to them. Through work one learns to find one's place in society. It is an educational activity with inherent potential for inclusion par excellence. Since work defines some achievable targets and creates a web of interdependence, it entails making efforts in a disciplined manner thus creating possibilities of greater self-control, focussing mental energies and keeping emotions under check. The value of work, particularly skills that involve good finish, is undervalued as a means of learning selfdiscipline. The discipline exercised by the material (say clay or wood one is working with) is more effective and qualitatively different from the discipline exercised by one human being on another. Work involves materials or interaction with other people (mostly both) thus creating possibilities of practical knowledge of natural substances and of relationships with people. All this is in addition to the usual physical skills involved in learning a trade that may be turned into a means of earning livelihood. The aspects of work mentioned here draw attention to the meaning making and knowledge construction dimension of work. This is the pedagogic function that work can play in the curriculum.

Benefits of this nature can be drawn from work only if it becomes **an integral part** of the school curriculum. In a majority of families in India, contributing to household work and family trade is a way of living. This pattern is changing due to the pressure of the school on children's time and the rampant competition in memorisation of information. The community of teachers and children could effortlessly graduate the practice of participation in household work to looking after one's own school. A well functioning and well maintained school offers ample opportunities for primary years of schooling, though that does not mean that all involvement with the work has to be only within the school premises. Integrating work with school curriculum would require a substantial amount of pedagogical understanding of how it would be integrated with learning and of evaluation. Schools at present are not geared for work as part of curriculum in terms of infrastructure as well. There no workshops. Even working with clay requires plain surface to work on. No practical activity can be initiated without the requisite preparation for it.

We also have to remember that work as forced labour is perhaps the most demeaning of all coercions. There have to be adequate measures in place to ensure that introduction of work as an integral part of curriculum should never lead to a situation where labour is thrust on unwilling children and its learning potential gets exhausted. Instead routine and repetitive activity is carried on for the sake of production or it gets associated with division of labour based on caste and gender. Also, a teacher making children work without himself participating in the work is unlikely to achieve the objectives of integrating work with curriculum. The inclusion of work within the school must also never allow justification of exploitation of children.

Pursued in an academic setting, work carries the remarkable potential of generating new forms of creativity and understanding while opening up the possibility of transforming the nature of work itself. Work is necessarily an interdisciplinary activity. Academic activity tends to be imprisoned within disciplinary boundaries. When academic learning and work are simultaneous and collocated there is a chance of greater creativity in academic pursuits as also in the methods and tools of doing work. A synergetic enhancement can take over. That is how efficient hand pumps were designed. In early days our high-flying polythene balloons used to burst while going through extremely cold stratosphere till a scientifically minded worker suggested that putting a little carbon powder in the fabric would help to keep it warm by absorbing sunlight. Indeed all the great inventors were tinkers who were not innocent of a little science. Edison, Ford and Faraday belonged to this category, so also those who built the first spectacles – or telescopes. There is little doubt that much of the traditional knowledge of our potters, craftsmen, weavers, farmers and medical men came through such pursuits – where the same persons were simultaneously engaged in physical work and academic thinking. We need to infuse such a culture in our education.

Institutionalising work in the school curriculum will require creative and bold thinking that breaks out of its stereotyped location in periods of Socially Useful and Productive Work about which all children and teachers are justifiably skeptical. It should be examined how the rich knowledge base and skills of manual work of marginalised children can be turned into a source of their own dignity as well as a source of learning for other children. This is especially important in the context of the growing alienation of the middle-upper class children from their cultural roots and the central role played by the education system in aggravating and accelerating this process. There is immense potential for utilising the knowledge base of the vast productive sections of society as a powerful means to transform the education system. Work seen as a form of 'valid' knowledge allows one to re-examine the invisibility of the contributions of women and non-dominant groups to what is regarded as valuable in society. Productive work would need to find a place at the centre of curriculum in order to act as a powerful corrective to the 'bookish', information-oriented and generally unchallenging character of school education and, in turn, help relate the latter to life needs of the child. Pedagogical experience in using work would become an effective and critical developmental tool at different stages of childhood and adolescence. Thus 'work-centered education' is different from vocational education.

The school curriculum from the pre-primary to senior secondary stage should be reconstructed to realise the pedagogic potential of work in *knowledge acquisition, developing values and multiple-skill formation.* As the child matures, a work-centred pedagogy can be pursued with increasing complexity but always enriched with the required flexibility and contextuality. A set of work-related generic competencies (basic, inter-personal and systemic) could be pursued at all stages of education. This includes critical thinking, transfer of learning, creativity, communication skills, aesthetics, work motivation, work ethic of collaborative functioning and entrepreneurship-cum-social accountability. For this evaluation parameters would also need to be redesigned. Without an effective and universal programme of work-centred education, it is unlikely that UEE (and later Universal Secondary Education too) would ever succeed.

3.7.1 Vocational Education and Training

We propose that we move in a phased manner towards a new programme of vocational education and training (VET), which is built on the bed-rock of a 10 to 12 year programme of work-centred education in the school, and which is structurally located outside the school. This programme needs to be conceived and implemented in a mission mode, involving the establishment of separate VET centres and institutions, integrating with and expanding the scope of existing institutions such as the ITIs, polytechnics, krishi vigyan kendras, primary health centres, engineering, agricultural and medical colleges, and cooperatives, etc. VET would be designed for all those children who wish to acquire additional skills or seek livelihoods through vocations. This would serve as a 'dignified' rather than terminal and 'last-resort' option. As with the school, these institutions would also be inclusive, providing for skill development of differentially-abled children along with others. A programme of career psychology and counseling as a development tool for children in the secondary and higher secondary stages would enable children to plan their movement towards who wish to join them.

The proposed VET could offer the following flexible and modular certificate or diploma courses for varying durations (including short durations) in livelihoods and/or vocations. These courses could be planned based on patterns of production, services and access to resources, in various geographic areas. These courses would have multiple entry and exit points and would also have horizontal and vertical linkages with academic and professional programmes. The VET centres would be established at block, district and major urban centres, making a variety of options accessible to those wishing to avail them.

The curriculum of such programmes should remain up-todate and flexible, if the programme is to serve as a viable way of learning skills rather than become moribund and irrelevant to vocations and professions. Centres in charge would need to have adequate resources as well as infrastructure and academic freedom to carve out 'work benches' (or 'work places') in the neighbourhood of agricultural and forest-based production centres utilizing the natural and human resources available. For this purpose, it should be obligatory for the private and public sector industries, especially for small industries and manufacturers, to provide opportunities for skill development, and skills and attitudes necessary for entrepreneurship and merchandising, to provide 'work benches' and mentoring support on the training site.

During the period of the SSA, until 2010 when UEE is achieved, the eligibility could be class V, but after this it could be made Class VIII certificate and eventually a class X certificate. In no case would children below the age of 16 be eligible for admission into the VET programmes.

VET centres could also act as craft and hobby centres for all children, right from primary schools, and could be accessed during or after school hours. Suitable ways of involving locally available skilled persons, such as craftspersons, mechanics, iron smiths, bamboo workers, etc. should be found so that they could participate as invited faculty. A creative, decentralized way of accrediting such expertmentors in the local areas would need to be evolved.

3.8 EDUCATION FOR PEACE

We live in an age of unprecedented violence with constant threats posed by intolerances, fanaticisms, disputes and discordances. Ethical action, peace and welfare are facing new challenges. The space for peace education in the framework of national school curriculum document is compellingly clear in the light of the escalating trends of, and taste for, violence globally, nationally and locally. Education is a significant dimension of the long-term process of building peace tolerance, justice, inter-cultural understanding and civic responsibility. However, education as practised in schools often promotes forms of violence both real and symbolic. In these circumstances, the need to reorient education and therefore the school curriculum takes priority. As a value, it cuts across all other curricular areas, and coincides and complements the values emphasized there-in. It is therefore a concern cutting across the curriculum and the concern of all teachers.

Education for peace seeks to nurture ethical development, with values, attitudes and skills required for living in harmony within oneself and with others including nature. It embodies joy of living and encompasses respect for human rights, justice, tolerance, cooperation, social responsibility, respect for cultural diversities, in addition to a firm commitment to democracy and resolving conflicts nonviolently. Hence the need for the development of a personality with inner resources of love, hope and courage. Peace education must be a concern that permeates the entire school life – curriculum, co-curriculum, classroom environment, school management, teacher-pupils relationship, teaching-learning processes and the entire gamut of school activities. Hence it is important to examine the curriculum and examinations from the point of view of how it may contribute to children's sense of inadequacy, frustration, impatience and insecurity. Also the need to consciously counter the negative influence of growing violence around, and its representation in the media, on the minds of children, and in its place promote a reflective engagement with deeper aspects living an ethical and peaceful life. Education in true sense should empower individuals to clarify their values; to enable them to take conscious and deliberate decisions, taking into cognisance the consequences of their actions; to choose the way of peace rather than violence; to enable them to be makers of peace rather than only of consumers of peace.

3.8.1 Strategies

Ethical development does not mean imposition of do's and don'ts, rather devising means and ways to help children learn to make choices and decide what is right, what is kind, what is best for the common good keeping in view the broader implications and personal and social values.

Children can understand almost everything they hear, but are often not able to reconcile contradictions between what is said and what is done. Even a minor disagreement at home can affect children very deeply. A state of permanent disaffection amongst elders or a disintegrating relationship between parents creates the kind of incalculable fear and depression that often manifest as aggression a few years later in early youth. There is need to bring parents and teachers together for more than only academic purposes. The responsibility of development personal ethics does not rest solely with either parents or with the school.

Ethical development follows a pattern characterizing different age group. During the primary years, children are yet exploring their immediate environment and developing consciousness of their own self. Their behaviour revolves around avoiding punishments and seeking rewards. They attach notions of good or bad, right or wrong depending upon what is approved or disapproved. At this stage, what they see in adults prompts them to construct their own understanding of ethical behaviour.

As children grow, though their reasoning capabilities are much better developed, yet they are not mature enough to question assumptions and norms. Inspired by the need to impress others and validate their self-image as strong and capable, they have the tendency to violate rules. At this stage, facilitating reflection on the basis of rules and the norms, restrictions, courtesies and obligations etc. through discussions and dialogues. produces insight into the linkage between collective good, value of restrain, sacrifice, compassion etc., which constitute the moral ways of being.

Still later, as abstract thinking is fully developed, individual can make well reasoned judgements about what constitutes ethical behaviour. This may lead to acceptance and internalisation of ethical principles which then can be sustained in the long run. Even in the absence of an external authority, ethically mature individuals behave in just and appropriate ways and understand the basis of rules, norms and how it contributes to the overall order and peace.

Our earliest and best teachers found stories and anecdotes the best way to get an important spiritual teaching or social message across. Along with this is the universal fact that every child no matter how dull or uninspired his home life, has something to say, some insight to contribute in a class discussion. The teacher needs to draw the class out, gain their confidence, and not use threatening language or hostile body language.

Teaching values has often meant exhortations about desirable behaviour. It has also meant suppression and denial of "undesireable" "unacceptable" feelings and desires. This often leads children to hide their own real feelings, desires, thoughts and convictions and simply pay lip service to moral values and ideals, without any commitment. Hence the need to move away from talk, to experiences and reflection, where no simplistic approach is taken to moral behaviour, but instead complex motivations and ethical dilemmas associated with human interest are explored and understood.

Teachers could make deliberate attempts to infuse and reinforce the importance of peace related values which commensurate with the textual material and the developmental stages of children. For example, teachers can take advantage of a hidden components in the lesson by using appropriate strategies to awaken positive feelings, experiences to reflect, explore, discover and construct understanding of peace related values. Strategies like questions, stories, anecdotes, games, experiments discussions, dialogues, value clarification, examples, analogies, metaphors, role play, and simulation are helpful in promoting peace through teaching-learning. The teaching and practice of ethics goes from the personal, to social and community-oriented thinking and links up with global perspectives. A teacher who is oriented to the perspective of peace can introduce such opportunities for reflecting at these scales, and their inter-linkages. Teacher education programmes could consider introducing peace education as an optional subject of study.

Schemes of Study and Assessment

'School' all over the country by and large refers to class I to X, extending to XII in some states, while in other classes XI and XII are regarded as pre-university or junior colleges. Some schools also include two to three years of pre-school classes. The breaking-up of schooling into four 'stages' is for more than administrative convenience. From the point of view of curriculum design and teacher preparation these stages have a developmental validity. Seen from a stage-wise perspective, curriculum thinking and school organization can overcome problems created by the current preoccupation with 'mono-grade' classrooms as being the norm, with rigid application of age-based grouping of children and class-wise teaching and learning objectives. Single and two teacher primary schools could be reconceptualised as a learning group with different abilities and learning needs, rather than as 'multigrade' classrooms requiring time management techniques. Assessing children for what they have learnt could also then take place over a longer cycle of years spent in school, rather than as yearly requirements spelt for each class, in hierarchical progression. This would allow more respect for children's pace of learning. Schemes such as the Minimum Levels of Learning reinforced not only the rigid adherence to year end outcomes, but allowed for these to be further narrowed to lessons. Describing the characteristics and concerns of the curriculum, pedagogy and assessment in stages allows syllabi, textbooks and learning resources, and for teachers to plan for children's development and the gradual and cumulative deepening of abilities, competencies and concepts.

3.9 SCHEMES OF STUDY

3.9.1 Early Childhood Education

The early childhood stage, until the age of six to eight years, is the most critical period when the foundations are laid for life-long development and the realization of full potential. It is the formative stage, influencing later attitudes and values as well the as the desire to learn. The philosophy of Early Childhood Care and Education (ECCE) is that young children must be provided carė, opportunities and experiences that lead to their all round development—physical, mental, social and emotional, and school readiness. The perspective is hence a holistic and integrated one that views health and nutritional needs of children as integrally related with their psycho-social/educational development. The curriculum framework and pedagogy for ECCE must be based this holistic perspective.

It is well-known that children have a natural desire to learn and make sense of the world around them. Learning in the early years must hence be directed by the child's interests and priorities and contextualised in her experiences rather that formally structured. An enabling environment for children would be one that is rich in stimulation and experiences, allows them to explore, experiment and freely express themselves and is embedded in social relations that give them a sense of warmth, security and trust. Play, music, rhyme, art and other activities along with opportunities for speaking, listening and expression are essential components of learning at this stage. It is important that the language used in early education is one that the child is familiar with. As children who come under the purview of ECCE are a heterogeneous group ranging from infants to pre-schoolers, it is important that activities and experiences for them are developmentally appropriate. For instance, for infants and toddlers, their surroundings must be stimulating to sensory experiences and allow for free movement while older children would need a lot of rhyme, rhythm, hands on activities and free expression.

Early identification of disabilities assessment and providing appropriate stimulation would go a long way in preventing the aggravation of disadvantage on this account. The caution would be against pressurizing children to write, 'learn lessons' and formally introducing them to English or a second language before they are ready for it, *i.e.* against making pre-schools into training centres for admission to primary schools. In fact the suggestion is that ECCE cover the age group 0-8 years (i.e so as to include the early primary school years). This is in order that the holistic perspective of ECCE and its methodologies (particularly all round and integrated development, activity-based learning, listening and speaking a language before learning to write it, contextuality, continuity between home and school and so on) can inform learning experiences of children throughout the childhood stage and lead to a smooth transition into the elementary school stage.

The ECCE programmes present a picture of plurality, with government, quasi government and private agencies providing a variety of services. However the coverage of these programmes is extremely narrow and the quality of services provided is variable and largely poor.

A vast majority of children, especially those belonging to poor and marginal groups are not covered by early care programmes and are left to fend for themselves. Pre-school programmes range from those that subject children to a dull and monotonous routine to where children are exposed to structured formal learning, taught English, made to do tests and homework and denied their right to play from an early age. These are undesirable and harmful practices that result from misguided parental aspirations and the growing commercialization of pre-schooling. However, such practices are detrimental to children's development and motivation to learn.

Good quality programmes for ECCE have a positive impact on children's all-round development. This in itself is reason enough to demand that all children have a right to early childhood care and education and it is hence unfortunate that the 0-6 age groups has been excluded from the purview of article 21. In addition it is also seen to have critical linkages with enrolment of children in schools and learning outcomes. To provide ECCE of equitable quality to all children, it is necessary that adequate funds are committed for this purpose. While there is need for decentralization, flexibility and contextuality in these programmes, there is urgent need to evolve appropriate norms and guidelines and a regulatory framework is set in place so that children's development is not compromised. Capacity building at all levels in relation to the plurality of roles that different functionaries play as well as appropriate/fair wages must also be ensured.

3.9.2 Elementary School

The period of elementary school, from Class I to Class VIII, is now also recognized as the period of compulsory schooling vide the Constitutional amendment making education a fundamental right. The beginning of this period marks the formal introduction of the child to reading, writing and arithmetic, culminating in the introduction of the formal disciplines such as the sciences and social sciences, towards the end of elementary school. This period of eight years is one of tremendous cognitive development and shaping of reason, intellect and social skills, and skills and attitudes necessary for work.

As the effort to achieve UEE is stepped up, the elementary school grades now cater to a vast variety of children of the school going age. Plurality and flexibility without compromising on standards needs to become the hallmark of education for this period. Education during this period must be of an integrated character, enabling children to acquire facility in language and expression and grow in confidence in themselves as learners, both within and outside school.

The first concern of the school is on the development of the child's language competence: articulation and literacyrelated, and to use language to create, to think and communicate with others. A special stress is needed on ensuring that there are maximum opportunities for those who wish to study in their mother tongue, including tribal languages and linguistic pockets, even if the numbers of students are small. The ability of the system to promote and nurture these options, along with working out mechanisms to ensure that future options remain open, would become a marker of its ability provide for quality education. To achieve this there must be a creative and concerted effort to maintain the multi-lingual genius of Indians, and implement the three language formula. While English may be taught during this period, it must not be at the expense of learning Indian languages.

The development of mathematical thinking, beginning with learning numeracy and moving towards enjoyment of and facility with more abstract ideas, needs to be supported with concrete experiences and work with manipulands. It is in the early years, up to class IV, that efforts at diagnosing learning difficulties and addressing remedial work in language and mathematics must be directed.

Such concrete experiences are also essential in introduction to the integrated study of the environment, through which children's intuitive knowledge of the world is integrated into school knowledge. Over the years, this study would move towards a more disciplinary approach, but with integrative themes, within which there are located opportunities to develop concepts, learn the vocabulary of the discipline and the methods.

The study of arts and crafts are essential ways of developing not only the aesthetic sensibility but also to learn to manipulate materials and develop attitudes and skills essential for work. The curriculum must expose children to practical life skills and work experiences of varied kinds. Physical development through sports activities is also a must. A variety of activities in this stage of schooling, including participating in cultural programmes, organizing events, travelling to places outside the school, provide experiences to develop socially and emotionally into a creative and confident person, sensitive to others, and capable of taking initiative and responsibility. The approach to the whole curriculum would need to be process oriented rather than outcome oriented. All these arenas of development should be made available to all children, including those with various kinds of impairments. Care must be taken to ensure that the curriculum does not reinforce stereotypes about preferences, choices and capabilities of different groups. In this context, the gradual inclusion of vocationally oriented skills as a part of exposure to work would be an important aspect of an inclusive curriculum.

3.9.3 Secondary School

Secondary school is a period of intense physical change and formation of identity. It is also the period of intense vibrancy and energy. The ability to reason with abstractions and use logic emerges, allowing children the possibility of deep engagement with both understanding and generating knowledge beyond the here and now. A critical understanding of the self in relation to society also emerges during this period. The courses at this level generally aim at creating the awareness of disciplines and introduces students to the possibilities and scope of study in them. Through such engagement, they also discover their own interests and aptitudes and begin to form ideas on what courses of work a and related study they might like to pursue later. For a large number of children, this is also a terminal stage, to leave school and begin developing productive work skills. For a large number of children for whom this stage becomes terminal on account of socio-economic circumstances, ___ need to be evolved to offer opportunities for learning creative and prospective work skills while the system as a whole moves towards universalizing secondary education. Providing access to libraries and experience in laboratories is essential, and there must be a concerted effort to ensure that all children have access to such facilities.

These two years are-shadowed by the **spectre of the 'board examination'**—marks in this examination determine future options. Schools often proudly state that they finish the entire syllabus for class X by the end of the first term, and spend the rest of the year (two terms) on revision, so that students are well prepared for their examination. Class IX of this stage, and later class XI are sacrificed for the same reason. This preoccupation with the examination, and its deleterious effect on learning needs to be reviewed and challenged. Is it worth wasting a year of perhaps the most fruitful period of a child's life in such non-productive engagement? Is it not possible that by pacing learning more evenly through the year, we may serve preparation for examination itself much better? On account of the examinations, many other curricular areas, especially sports and arts, are also compromised. It is necessary to ensure that these areas are protected, and also that serious attempt is made to institute meaningful experiences of work during this period.

Most boards in the country offer limited or no optional courses in this period: two languages (one of which is English), mathematics, science and social sciences are the typical examination subjects. In this group, the courses of mathematics and English which are responsible for 'failure' of a large number of students need to be revisited, and redesigned. The **policy of declaring pass-fail** in the whole examination, and the meaning of 'pass mark' may also need to be reviewed. Related issues are discussed in chapter 6 the section on systemic reforms.

A few boards encourage students to also choose an **optional course** from a range which includes economics, music and cookery. Such options could be increased and the possibilities of substituting the more traditional disciplines with these options could also be considered. **Vocational options** could also be introduced. Many such vocational options may arise from the world of productive work in the local community. For example auto maintenance in garages, tailoring and paramedical services offer possibilities for collaboration to create meaningful vocational courses; school boards could accredit such learning and thereby also recognize the numerable sites of learning which are situated outside school. In our country, many vocational stream courses have deteriorated in their quality and hence are unable to provide students with meaningful work related knowledge and skills. In many cases, these courses like routine credentialing courses, and making no difference between learning to do a job vs. learning to get a job.

3.9.4 Higher Secondary School

The status of the academic and vocational streams in higher secondary school need to be reviewed, in view of the continued preoccupation with and influence of the board and entrance examinations and in view of the continued privilege given to the so-called 'academic stream' and the failure of the 'vocational stream' to take off. This period of two years is one where students make choices based on their interests, aptitudes and needs regarding the future life.

The **possibilities of choosing optional courses** of study to explore and understand different areas of knowledge, both in relation to one's interest and one's future career is integral to this stage. Exploring disciplines and approaching problems and issues from rich interdisciplinary perspectives are possible in this stage. There is need to allow for such investigations to take place between and outside the 'subjects' chosen for study.

Most boards of study offer a variety of subject areas, in addition to compulsory courses of language. There is concern about the formal or informal restrictions that operate to restrict the choices of subjects of study for the students. Several boards restrict the combinations in the form of 'science stream', 'arts stream' and 'commerce stream'. The CBSE does not restrict the possibility combinations that students can choose, but in view of the increasing popularity of some combinations of subjects of studies, and also a perception of status of subjects in relation to each others, many such options are now foreclosed to students. Further,

Universities also need to review their admission criteria as they currently restrict admissions based on the kinds and combinations of courses studied in the +2 stage. As a consequence, many significant and meaningful combinations of study, such as, for example, physics, mathematics and philosophy, or literature, biology and history, are closed to students.

Recent trends of schools tailoring their classes to medical and engineering courses has led to an artificial restriction on the courses they offer in the school, arguably on grounds of popularity and time-tabling. In many parts of the country, students who want to study arts and liberal subjects are left with very few options. Schools also discourage students from opting for unconventional combinations, often on account of time-tabling considerations. We believe it is essential to keep all options open for students. In case there are not enough students in a school opting for a particular subjects, schools could consider working out arrangements with other schools in the neighbourhood, so that they could employ a resource teacher together. Such resource teachers could also be employed at the block level to teach such special subjects that would not otherwise be available in the school. School boards may also consider a more active role in promoting subjects and streams of study.

The courses offered in the +2 stage need to be alive to developments in the disciplines, as new knowledge areas are carved out, disciplinary boundaries shift and multidisciplinary studies develop. To allow students to engage with areas of study which are growing in importance within the disciplines and fields, courses could also be designed to offer optional modules, rather than trying to cover everything and packing courses too much. For example, history could have an optional module to study either archeology, or world history; similarly physics could offer options of astronomy, space science and rocketry, etc. or so that optional modules of study are available within the courses.

Under pressure to 'cover' vast syllabi, many important aspects of learning such as practicals and field trips, and ways of learning such as reference work, project work and presentations, are not fully utilised, to the detriment of overall learning. Well equipped **laboratories and libraries and access to computers** are essential, and all effort must be made to ensure that schools and junior colleges are well equipped with such resources.

The vocational stream originally was meant to address the needs of those who would enter into work earlier than those would enter into professions via academic streams, or pursue study and research. We recommend the **merging of the vocation and academic streams** for three reasons. First, the changing nature of vocations itself needs a more flexible and robust curriculum which lays more 'academic' foundations of knowledge and skills of the vocation, by drawing on related disciplines. Second, those studying in the academic streams could also keep their own options more open by opting for and studying related vocational courses. Finally, the goal of providing opportunities for horizontal and vertical mobility may be realized if there is only one stream, rather than two. In the long run the inter-linkages with these options and the proposed VET may be evolved.

Given the developmental qualities of this stage, **guidance and counseling** by trained professionals must be made available to children. Interventions to enhance career awareness, career exploration and planning are also very essential. Continued opportunities for **sports and cultural activities** through youth clubs and other such fora must be provided to enrich the life-scape of children in this period. Such facilities could be made available at least at the block level, to provide services and information.

3.9.5 Open Schooling and Bridge Schooling

Beginning with the National Open School, open school boards which have begun to function in a few states now are able to provide much more flexibility and options for students. The range of subjects they offer is wide. With more flexibility in examination taking, and the possibility of credit transfer from other boards, the open schools have been able to provide a more humane approach to the processes of certification. Knowledge about and access to open school could be more widely disseminated, along with efforts to address misconceptions regarding equivalence with other board examinations. By holding these examinations more closely along with other board examination, it would also be possible to ensure that students do not lose a school year.

Bridge courses are conducted widely in many parts of the county to enable children who are out of school to study in programmes and become integrated into classes suitable to their age. In the medium term it is essential to have well conceived programmes that are able to meet this curricular objective. Anything less than this would exacerbate the deprivation that these children have already suffered, and constitute a flagrant disregard of their rights. Rigorous research and development of the pedagogy and materials required for such programmes to succeed, stringent implementation norms and provisioning of facilities, as well as continued academic and social support for these children, after they have been placed in schools, is absolutely essential.

3.10 ASSESSMENT AND EVALUATION

In Indian education, the term evaluation is associated with examination, stress and anxiety. All efforts at curriculum definition and renewal come to naught if they cannot engage with the bulwark of the evaluation and examination system embedded in schooling. We are concerned about the ill effects that examinations have on efforts to make learning and teaching meaningful and joyous for children. Currently the board examinations negatively influence all testing and assessment through the school years, beginning with pre-school. At the same time a good evaluation and examination system can become an integral part of the learning process and benefit both learners themselves, and the educational system by giving credible feedback. This section begins with addressing evaluation and assessment as they are relevant to the normal course of teaching learning in the school, as a part of the curriculum. Issues relating to the examination system and in particular to the board examinations are separately addressed in chapter V.

3.10.1 The Purpose of Assessment

Education is concerned with preparation for meaningful life, and evaluation should be a way of providing credible feedback on the extent to which we are successful in implementing such an education. Seen from this perspective, current processes of evaluation, which measure and assess a very limited range of faculties are highly inadequate and do not provide a complete picture of an individual's abilities or progress towards aims of education.

But even this limited purpose of evaluation, of providing feedback on scholastic and academic development, can be achieved only if the teacher is prepared even before the course of teaching, with not only the techniques of assessment but also the parameters for evaluation and kinds of tools that will be employed. In addition to judging the quality of the student's achievement, a teacher would also need to collect, analyse and interpret performance on various items of the assessment to come to an understanding of the extent and nature of students' learning in different domains. The purpose of assessment is necessarily to improve the teaching learning process and materials, and be able to review the objectives that have been identified for different school stages, by gauging the extent to which capabilities of the learners have been developed. Needless to say, this does not mean that tests and examinations will have to be conducted frequently. On the contrary, routine activities and exercises can be employed effectively to assess learning.

Well-designed assessment and regular report cards provide learners with feedback, and set standards for them to strive towards. They also serve to inform parents on the quality of learning and development of their wards. This is not a means to encourage competition; if one is looking for quality in education, then segregating and ranking children and injecting them with feelings of inferiority cannot do it.

Last, credible assessment provides a report, or certifies the completion of a course of study, providing other schools and educational institutions, the community and prospective employers with information regarding the quality and extent of learning.

The popular notion that evaluation can lead to identifying needs of remediation, to be attended to with remedial teaching, has created many problems in curriculum planning. The term remediation needs to be restricted to specific special programmes that enable children who are having a problem with literacy/reading (associated with reading failure and later with comprehension) or numeracy (especially the symbolic aspects of mathematical computation and place value). Teachers require specific training for effective diagnostic testing that can be of assistance in remediation efforts. Similarly, remedial work would require specifically developed materials and planning so that the teacher is able to give one-on-one time to work with the child, beginning with what she/he knows and moving to what he/she needs to learn, through a continuous process assessment through careful observation. Indiscriminate usage of the term distracts from the general problems of effective pedagogy, and make the child solely responsible for his or her learning and also learning 'failure'.

3.10.2 Assessing Learners

A meaningful report on the quality and extent of a child's learning needs to be comprehensive. A curriculum where creativity, innovativeness, and development of the whole being, the hallmark, makes uniform tests which assess memorized facts and textbook based learning obsolete. We need to redefine and search for new parameters for and ways of evaluation and feedback. In addition to the learner's achievements in specific subject areas which lend themselves easily to testing, assessment would need to encompass attitudes to learning, interest and ability to learn independently.

3.10.3 Assessment in the Course of Teaching

Preparing report cards is a way for the teacher to think about each individual child and review what he or she has learnt during the term, and what she needs to work on and improve. To be able to write such report cards, teachers would need to think about each individual child and hence pay attention to them during their everyday teaching and interactions. One does not need special tests for this—activities of learning themselves provide the basis for such ongoing observational, qualitative assessments of children. Maintaining daily diary based on observation helps in continuous and comprehensive evaluation. An extraction from the diary of a teacher for a week mentions the following: "*Kiran enjoyed his work. He took an instant liking to the books that were informative and brief. He says that he likes simple and clear language. In noting down facts, he goes for short answers. He says that it helps him understand things easily. He favours a practical approach.*" Similarly, keeping samples and notes of the child's work at different stages provides both the teacher and the learner herself or himself with a systematic record of their learning progress. The belief that assessment must lead to finding learning difficulties to then be remediated is often very impractical and not founded on sound understanding of pedagogic practice. Problems regarding conceptual development cannot and do not wait for formal tests in order to be detected. A teacher can, in the course of teaching itself, come to know of such problems, during which through methods of asking questions that make children think or giving them small assignments. She can then attend to them in the process of teaching—by ensuring that her planning is flexible and responsive to the learners and their learning.

3.10.4 Curricular Areas that Cannot be 'Tested for Marks'

Each area of the curriculum may not lend itself to being 'tested'; it may even be antithetical to the nature of learning in the curricular area. This includes areas such as work, physical education, music and art. Currently this has the effect of making these subjects and activities 'less important' in the curriculum; these areas are inadequately provided for in terms of material resources and curricular planning, and marked by a lack of seriousness. Further, time allocated for them is also frequently sacrificed to accommodate special classes. This is a serious compromise of parts of the curriculum of deep educational significance and potential. Even if 'marks' cannot be given, children can be assessed for their development in these areas. Participation, interest, and level of involvement, extent to which abilities and skills have been honed are some markers which can help teachers to gauge the benefits of what children learn and gain through such activities. Asking children to self report on their learning can also provide teachers with insight into children's educational progress and give them feedback on improving curriculum or pedagogy.

3.10.5 Design and Conduct of Assessment

Assessments and examinations must be credible, and based on valid ways of gauging learning.

As long as examinations and tests test children's ability to remember and recall textbook knowledge, all attempts to redirect the curriculum towards learning will be thwarted. First, tests in knowledge-based subject areas must be able to gauge what children have learnt, and their ability to use this knowledge for problem solving and applications. In addition, they must also be able to test the processes of thinking to gauge if the learner has also learnt where to find information, how to use new information, and to analyse and evaluate the same.

Types of questions that are set for assessment need to go beyond what is given in the book. So often children's learning is restricted as teachers do not accept their answers if they are different from what is presented in the guide books.

Questions that are open-ended and challenging could also be used. Designing good test items and questions is an art and teachers should spend time thinking about and devising such questions. The interest and ability of teachers to design good questions can be promoted through district or state level competitions. All questions papers must be designed graded for difficulty, to permit all children to experience a level of success, and to gain confidence in their ability to answer and solve.

Trying to devise good open-book examination can be a challenge that we must try to take up in our curricular efforts at all levels of school. This would require teachers and examination setters to emphasise the interpretation of and application of learning, over the arguments and facts that can be located in the book. There have been successful demonstrations that such examinations can be carried out on a large scale, and that teachers can themselves be trusted with moderating the results of such examinations. So also, the assessment of projects and lab work can be made credible and sound.

It is important that after receiving their corrected papers, children rewrite the answers and these are again reviewed by the teachers to ensure that children have learnt, and gained something out of the ordeal.

Competition is motivating, but it is an extrinsic rather than intrinsic form of motivation. It is of course much easier to establish and to manipulate, and therefore frequently resorted to by teachers and school systems as a way creating and nurturing the drive for excellence. Schools begin 'ranking' children even from their pre-primary years, as a way of inculcating in them a competitive spirit. Such a competitive drive has several negative side-effects on learning—often superficial learning is sufficient to create and maintain impressions, over time students lose their ability to take initiative or do things from one's own interest, areas that cannot be 'marked' become neglected. This has unhealthy consequences for classroom culture, making children individualistic and unsuited to team work. There is an absurd importance given to term examinations and an unnecessary focus on them, often with extreme arrangements of invigilation and secrecy. While the physical and psychological effects of this may not be readily visible till middle school, they frequently lead to high levels of stress in children, and cause early burn out. Schools and teachers need to ask themselves whether there is really much to be gained out of such practices and to what extent learning requires such systems of marking and ranking.

3.10.6 Self-assessment and Feedback

The role of the assessment is to gauge the progress that the learner and teacher have made towards achieving the aims that have been set and appraising how this could be done better. Opportunity for feedback, leading to revision and improvement of performance should constantly be available without exams and evaluation being used as a threat to study.

Grading and correction carried out in the presence of students and providing feedback on the answers they got right and wrong, and why. Asking children about why they answered what they did, assists teachers in going beyond the written answer to engage with children's thinking. Such processes also take away the frightening judgmental quality of marks in a test, and enable children to understand and focus on their mistakes and learning through these mistakes. Sometimes head teachers object, claiming that correction in the presence of the child reduces 'objectivity'. This is a misplaced concern for 'objectivity' stemming from a competitive system that believes in judging children. Such a concern for 'objectivity' is misplaced in evaluation which is consistent with educational goals.

Not only learning outcomes, but learning experiences themselves must be evaluated. Learners happily comment on the totality of their experience. Exercises, both individual and group, can be designed to enable them to reflect on and assess their learning experiences. Such experiences also provide them with self regulatory capabilities essential for 'learning to learn'. Such information is also valuable feedback to the teacher, and can be used to modify the learning system as a whole.

Every classroom interaction with the children would require their evaluation of their own work, discussion with them of what should be tested and what are the ways to find out whether the competencies are being developed or not. Even very young children are able to give correct assessment of what they can or cannot do well. The role of teaching is to provide opportunity to each one to learn to the best of her ability and provide learning experiences which are for the development of cognitive qualities, physical well being and athletic qualities, as also affective and aesthetic qualities.

Report cards need to present to children and parents a comprehensive and holistic view of the child's development in many fields. Teachers must be able to say things about each child/student, which conveys to them a sense of individualized attention, reaffirms a positive self image, and communicates personal goals for them to work towards. Whether it is marks or grades that are reported, a qualitative statement by the teacher is necessary to support the assessment. Only through such a relationship with each child can any teacher succeed in influencing them, and contributing to their learning. Along with the teacher assessing each child, each could also assess him or herself and include this self-assessment in the report card.

Currently, many report cards carry information on subject areas, and have nothing to say about other aspects of children's development including their health, physical fitness and abilities in games, social skills and abilities in art and craft. Qualitative statements about these aspects of children's education and development would provide a more holistic assessment of educational concerns.

3.10.7 Areas that Require Fresh Thinking

There are many areas of the curriculum that can be assessed but for which we still do not have reliable and efficient instruments. This includes assessing learning that is carried out in groups, and learning in areas such as theatre, work and craft where skills and competencies develop over longer time scales and require careful observation.

Continuous and comprehensive evaluation has frequently been cited as the only meaningful kind of evaluation. This also requires much more careful thinking through when it is to be employed in a system effectively. Such evaluation places a lot of demand on teachers' time and ability to maintain meticulous records, if it is to be meaningfully executed and if it is to have any reliability as an assessment. If this simply increases stress on children by making all their activities into items for assessment, or making them experience the teacher's 'power', then it defeats the purpose of education. Unless a system is adequately geared for such assessment, it is better for teachers to engage in more limited forms of evaluation, but incorporating into it more features that will make the assessment a meaningful record of learning.

Finally the need to evolve and maintain credibility in assessment so that they perform their function of providing feedback, meaningfully.

3.10.8 Assessment at Different Stages

ECCE and classes I and II of the Elementary Stage: At this stage assessment must be purely qualitative judgements of children's activities in various domains and an assessment of the status of the health and physical development, based on observations through everyday interactions. On no account should they be made to take any form of test, oral or written.

Class III to class VIII of Elementary Stage: A variety of methods may be used, including oral and written tests and observations. Children should be aware that they are being assessed, but this must be seen by them as a part of the teaching process and not as a fearful constant threat. Grades or marks along with qualitative judgments of achievement and areas requiring attention are very essential at this stage. Children's own self-evaluation can also be a part of the report card from class V onwards. Rather than examinations, there could be short tests from time to time, which are criterion based. Term wise examinations could be commenced from class VII onwards when children are more psychologically ready to study large chunks and prepare, and to spend a few hours in an examination, working at answering questions.

Again the progress card must indicate besides general observations on health and nutrition specific observations on the overall progress of the learner for information and advice to the parents.

Secondary and Higher Secondary Stage (Class IX to XII): Assessment may be based more on tests, examinations and project reports, for the knowledge-based areas of the curriculum, along with self assessment. Other areas would be assessed via observation and also through self evaluation.

Reports could be presented along with much more analysis provided to the student regarding various skill/knowledge areas, and percentile, etc. This would assist them in understanding areas of study that they need to focus on and also help them by providing a basis for further choices they make regarding what to study further.

OBSERVATIONS

Three Language Formula—There was no need to revise the old controversy regarding the working of the three Language Formula. 'Let sleeping dogs lie.'

The document advocate that mother-tongue should be the medium of instruction in schools. This insistence is not practically sound.

Vocational Education and Training—It is stated that Vocational Education and Training (VET) needs to be conceived and implemented in a mission mode, involving the establishment of separate VET centres and institutions, integrating with and expanding the scope of existing institutions such as the ITIs, polytechniques, Krishi Vigyan Kendras, primary health centres, engineering, agricultural and medical colleges and cooperatives, etc. VETs is to be designed for all those children who wish to acquire additional skills or seek livelihood through education. This needs careful consideration as it is a radical departure from the present concept of vocationalisation of secondary education.

It is stated in the document that in no case would children below the age of 16, be eligible for admission into VET programmes. This implies that eighth pass students would have no provision for joining vocational education and training centres.

The recommendations of VET seem to be quite confusing.

The document recommends the merging of the vocational and academic stream. This needs a detailed discussion at various levels.

Observations on assessment need no comment as the issue has been discussed in detail at various forums. The Central Board of Secondary has initiated several desirable steps in this direction.

5

School and Classroom Environment

School and Classroom Environment is the chapter 4 of the draft and observations on it are given after its contents.

Learning takes place within a web of social relationships as teachers and pupils interact both formally and informally. Schools are institutional spaces for communities of learners, including both students and teachers. Play and scuffle with one's friends on the school grounds, free time to sit on the benches and chat with one's friends during breaks, gathering together for morning assembly and other festive and significant occasions in the school, studies carried out in the classroom, anxious turning of pages before a class test, and trips made with one's classmates and teachers to places outside the school all these are activities bring the community together, giving it the character of a learning community. Behind the scenes, but still significant in giving the school its character are the teachers and the head master, planning and carrying out daily routines, examinations and special events that mark the school calendar. How can we organize the environment in the school and classroom so that such interactions support and enhance both teaching and learning? How can the space of the school be nurtured as a context where children feel safe, happy and wanted, and which teachers find meaningful and professionally satisfying? The physical and psychological dimensions of the environment are important and are interrelated. In this chapter we examine these environments to understand how they significantly influence children's learning.

4.1 THE PHYSICAL ENVIRONMENT

Children are constantly interacting with the physical environment of their schools during structured or unstructured time, consciously or unconsciously. Yet not enough attention is paid to the importance of physical environment for learning. Often classrooms are overcrowded, with no alternative spaces to learn, nor are they attractive, inviting or sensitive towards children's needs. Inappropriate school design may drastically affect the teacher's productive output and classroom management. In fact, the role of this all encompassing, physical environment has been restricted merely to shelter the educational activity.

When children are asked about the kind of spaces they like, very often they want to be in a place that is colourful, friendly peacefuk and playful with lot of open space with small nooks and corners, animals, plants, flowers, trees, and toys. In order to attract and retain the children, the school environments must have these in and around them.

Classrooms can be brightened up by first ensuring adequate natural light inside and then made lively by placing children's work on display on the walls of the classroom and in different parts of the school. Drawings, art and craftwork put up on the walls and shelves give powerful message to children and their parents that their work is appreciated. This must be put at locations and heights that are physically and visually comfortably accessible to the children various age ranges in the school. Many of our schools continue to run in dilapidated and dingy buildings, presenting a dull, drab and un-stimulating physical setting. This can be changed with simple innovations, with combined efforts of school teachers, administrators and architects.

Buildings are the most expensive physical assets of the school. Maximum educational value should be derived from them. Creative and practical solutions can be used to maximize this educational value while repairing or upgrading existing schools or making new buildings. The enhancement of physical environment through this can bring about not just a cosmetic change but an inherent transformation in the way physical space connects with the pedagogy and the child. In many parts of the country, the school and classrooms have large permanent displays painted on the walls. Such visuals are over stimulating with time they become monotonous, and cease to enhance the quality of the space. Instead smaller sized, judiciously chosen murals may be a better way of adding colour to the school. Most of the wall display area should be utilized for children's own work, or charts made by the teacher, and these should be replaced about about a month. Preparing such wall displays and participating in putting them up can be also valuable learning activities for children.

Many schools have rather than playgrounds for outdoor learning activities. This compromises the quality of learning provided through the curriculum.

Ensuring that minimum requirements of infrastructure and materials are available, and supporting flexible planning that will help achieve curricular aims are important features that heads of school, cluster and block functionaries should focus on in their support to teachers. This applies to almost all aspects of school life. The many new pedagogies that have been promoted through efforts such as the DPEP have all suggested that the physical layout of the classroom could be altered so that children can sit together in small groups, or gather in a large circle for story telling, or sit on their own to carry out some individual reading or writing tasks, or assemble in a group near the radio or TV for a broadcast. For this, the arrangement of desks and chairs, benches and *daris could be altered.* Many schools have begun to acquire simple furniture that is suitable for such flexible organization. Single small *chowkis*, or desks and chairs for individual or pairs of children and *daris* are well suited for such classrooms, and could be adapted or altered to suit the needs of children with disability. But still many schools invest in heavy metal benches and long desks which can only be placed in rows, and which reinforce the teacher and black board-centred system of learning. Worse still, many of these do not have adequate place for children to keep their books and belongings, nor are they wide enough or with back supports suitable for the physical comfort of the child. Such furniture should be banned from school spaces.

The maximum use can be made of available school and classroom spaces as pedagogic resources. In some areas, the walls of the primary school classrooms till about 4 feet have been painted black so that they serve as a free slate, drawing board for children. In some schools geometric designs which can be used for activities are painted on the floor. A corner of the room may be used to organize learning materials, to keep some appropriate story books, puzzle or riddle cards and other self-access learning materials. When some children have finished their assigned lessons early, they can feel free to come and pick up something from this corner to occupy themselves.

Children can be encouraged to participate in activities to make the school and classroom attractive for study, work and play. Most government schools have the healthy practice of giving children the charge of cleaning, thereby encouraging the inclusion of work into the routine of the school. But it is also distressing to note that there are schools where it is the girls or the children coming from lower castes who are expected to do this work. In elite schools children do not take on any such responsibilities, and cleaning activities are often meted out as 'punishments' for misdemeanours. Such practices stem from and reinforce cultural norms of the division of labour on gender lines, and the association of distasteful jobs with traditional hereditary occupations of lower caste groups. As schools are public spaces that must be informed by values of equality as well as respect for labour/

work of all kinds, it is important that teachers consciously avoid distributing tasks on the basis of cultural notions. On the other hand keeping the classroom clean and putting things in place are important curricular experiences through which children learn to take individual and collective responsibility and to keep their classrooms and schools as attractive as possible. The understanding of being part of a larger collective, and the abilities needed to work within a collective can be internalized in children in a variety of ways as they interact in groups within the classroom and school.

4.2 NURTURING AN ENABLING ENVIRONMENT

As public spaces, schools must be marked by the values of equality, social justice and respect for diversity, as well as of the dignity and rights of children. These values must be consciously made part of the perspective of the school and form the foundation of school practice. An enabling learning environment is one where children feel secure, where there is absence of fear and is governed by relationships of equality and space for equity. Often this does not require any special effort on the part of the teacher, except to practise equality and not discriminate among children. Teachers should also nurture their classroom spaces as ones where children freely ask questions, engage in a dialogue with the teacher as well as their peers, during an ongoing lesson. Unless they can share their related experiences, clarify their doubts and ask questions, they will not engage with learning. If, instead of ignoring children's comments or sealing their tongues with strict rules of silence and restriction on the language to be used, teachers encouraged children to talk, they would find that the classroom is a more lively place and that teaching is not predictable and boring, but an adventure of interacting minds. Such an environment will facilitate the self confidence and self esteem of learners of all ages; it will also go a long way in improving the quality of learning itself.

Teachers and children are part of a larger society where identities based on membership of caste, gender, religious and linguistic group as well as economic status informs social interaction though this varies in different social, cultural and regional contexts. Tribal and dalit communities, members of minority groups and women are usually placed in situations of disadvantage because of their identities and are denied equal access to valued resources in society and participation in different institutions. Research on school processes suggests that identities of children continue to influence their treatment within schools thereby denying them meaningful and equal opportunities to learn. As part of the experience of schooling children also receive implicit messages through interpersonal relations, teacher attitudes and norms and values that are part of the culture of the school. These often reinforce notions of purity and pollution in relation to social hierarchies, desirable qualities of 'masculinity' and 'feminity' and privilege in certain ways of living, mainly that of the urban middle class, while rendering all others invisible. Children belonging to dalit and lower caste groups, and other socially discriminated groups such as sex workers and parents with HIV, are often subjected to demeaning treatment within the classroom, not only by teachers (often from higher caste and class) but also by their peers. Girls are often subject to stereotypical expectations based on notions of their future roles as wives and mothers rather than enabling them to develop their capabilities and claim their rights. Children with disability often confront insensitive environments where their needs are completely ignored. Schools must be conscious of the importance of creating equitable classroom environments in which students are not differentiated and subjected to unfair treatment and denied opportunities on their basis of their gender or membership of a caste, tribe or minority group. On the other hand the culture of the school must be one that highlights students identities as 'learners' and creates an environment that enhances the potential and interests of each child.

4.3 PARTICIPATION OF ALL CHILDREN

Opportunities to display talents, and share with peers are powerful facilities in nurturing motivation and involvement of children. It gives them the feeling of belonging to a community where they matter. Therefore it is all the more important that all children have such opportunities. In our schools we tend to select some children over and over again. While this small group benefits from the opportunities, becoming more self confident and visible in the school, other children experience repeated disappointment and progress through school with a constant wish for recognition and peer approval, that some teacher would think of also asking them to display their talents. Excellence and ability may be singled out for appreciation, but at the same time, opportunities need to be given to all children and their specific abilities recognized and appreciated. This includes children with disabilities, who may need assistance or more time to complete their assigned tasks. It would be even better if, while planning for such activities, the teacher discussed them with all the children in the class, and ensure that each child is given an opportunity to contribute. When planning, therefore, teachers must pay special attention to ensuring participation of all. This would become a marker of their effectiveness as teachers.

4.3.1 Competitiveness

Excessive emphasis on competitiveness and individual achievement is beginning to mark many of our schools, especially private schools catering to the urban middle classes. Very often as soon as children join, houses are allocated to them. Thereafter, almost every activity in the school is counted for marks that go into house points adding up to an end of year prize. Such 'house loyalties' seem to have the superficial effect of getting all children involved and excited about winning points for their houses, but this also distorts educational aims, where excessive competitiveness promotes doing better than someone else as an aim, rather than excelling on one's own terms and for the satisfaction of doing something well. Often placed under the monitoring eye of other children, this system distorts social relations within schools, adversely affecting peer relations and undermining values such as cooperation and sensitivity to others. School teacher groups need to reflect on the extent to which they want the spirit of competition to enter into and permeate every aspect of school life—performing more of a function to regulate and discipline than to nurture learning and interest.

Schools also undermine the diversity of capabilities and talents of children by categorizing them very early, on narrow cognitive criteria. Instead of relating to each child as an individual, early in their lives children are placed on cognitive berths in the classroom: the 'stars', the average, the below average and the 'failures'; most often they never have a chance to get off their berth by themselves. The demonizing effect of such labeling is devastating on children. Schools go to absurd lengths to make children internalize these labels, through verbal name calling such as 'dullards', segregating them in seating arrangements and even creating markers that visually (blazers and badges) divide children into achievers and those that are unable to perform. The fear of not having the right answer keeps many children silent in the classroom, thus denying them an equal opportunity to participate and learn. Equally paralyzed by the fear of failure are the so called achievers, who lose their capacity to try out new things from the fear of failure, of doing less well in examinations, and of losing their ranks. It is important to allow errors and making mistakes to remain an integral part of the learning process and remove the fear of not achieving 'full marks'. The school needs to send out a strong signal into the community of parents who pressurize children from an early age to be perfectionists. Instead of spending time in tuitions or at home to learn the 'perfect answers', parents need to encourage their children to spend their time reading story books, playing, doing reasonable amount of home work and revision. Instead of looking for courses on stress management for their pupils. School heads and school managements need to destress their curricula, and advise parents to destress children's life outside the school.

Schools which emphasize intense competitiveness must not be treated as examples by others, including state-run schools. The ideal of common schooling advocated by the Kothari Commission four decades ago continues to be valid as it reflects the values enshrined in our Constitution. Schools will succeed in inculcating these values only if they create an ethos in which every child feels happy and relaxed. This ideal is all the more relevant now because the system is approaching the universalization of elementary education, which implies that millions of first-generation learners are being enrolled. To retain them, the system – including its private sector – must recognize that there are many childhoods, that no single norm of capacity, personality or aspiration can serve in the emerging scenario. Those in-charge school administrators and teachers should also realize that when boys and girls from different socioeconomic and cultural backgrounds and different levels of ability study together, the class room ethos gets richer and more inspiring.

4.4 DISCIPLINE IN THE SCHOOL

School rules, norms and conventions define permitted 'good' and 'proper behaviour' for individual and groups of students. Maintaining discipline in schools is usually the prerogative of teachers, (often the sports master and administrators)—all adults in positions of authority. Frequently they also induct children as 'monitors' and 'prefects' and delegate this responsibility of maintaining 'order' and ensuring control. Punishment and reward play an important role in this. Those who implement rarely question the rules, or the implications that ensuring compliance may have for children's overall development, self-esteem and also their interest in learning. Forms of disciplining such as corporal punishment, verbal and non-verbal abuse of children continue to feature in many schools, and are used to humiliate children in front of their peers. Yet many teachers and even parents still believe that such punishment is important, unaware of the immediate and long term detrimental effects of these practices.

It is important for teachers to reflect on the rationale that underlie rules and conventions that govern schools, and whether these are consistent with our aims for education. For instance rules such as the length of the socks and the whiteness of the sports shoes are of no educationally defensible importance. Rules regarding maintaining silence in classrooms, answering 'one at time' and answering only if you know the right answer, can go against the values of equality and equal opportunity. Such rules may also discourage processes that are integral to children's learning, the development of a sense of community among peers though they may make the class 'easy to manage' for the teacher, and facilitate 'covering the syllabus'.

Inculcating the value/habit of self-discipline is important for the systematic pursuit of learning and development of the child's interests and potential. Discipline must enable performance of, and be conducive to, the task at hand, with rigour. It should enable freedom, choice and autonomy of the teacher and child. It is possible to involve children themselves in evolving rules, so that they understand the rationale for a rule, and feel a sense of responsibility in ensuring that they are followed. This way they would also learn the process of participating in decision making and democratic functioning. Similarly, mechanisms for conflict resolution between teachers and students and among students could also be evolved by the children themselves. The teacher should ensure that there are as few rules as possible, and that only rules that can be reasonably followed are created. It does no one any good to humiliate children for breaking rules, particularly when there are good reasons for the rule being broken. For instance 'noisy classrooms' are frowned upon by teachers as well as headmasters; but it is possible that rather than the noise being evidence that the teacher is not in control, it may be evidence of a lively participatory class.

Similarly head masters can be unreasonably strict about punctuality. A child who is late for an examination on account of a traffic jam must not be peanalised, and yet we find such rules being imposed in the name of higher values. Unreasonableness on the part of authorities in matters such as rules can demoralize children, their parents and also teachers. It may help to remember to first ask a child why he or she broke a rule, to listen to what they have to say, and then act accordingly. It is befitting a school head or teacher to exercise authority, rather than power. Arbitrariness and unreasonableness are characteristics of power, and are feared not respected.

4.5 SPACE FOR PARENTS AND COMMUNITY

The school is a structured space for guided learning, but the process of constructing knowledge is a continuous one, which goes on even outside the school. Typically schools make an effort to give children homework—school learning related work to be carried out at home. For younger children it is expected that parents will assist, but with older children homework is meant to be done most often on their own. In many schools teachers simply ask children to repeat what they have learnt in school, or answer questions taken from the book, or complete things they could not finish in the classroom. Teachers of children whose parents are not schooled often then complain that the parents cannot assist and support children. In fact the spread of tuitions among the poor is partly a result of the need to 'complete homework' in order to avoid punishment in school. If learning is continuous, to be carried on after school also, then homework could be planned differently. It need not depend on parents reinforcing what the school has already done. It could set different kinds of activities for children to do, on their own or with parents. This could also provide opportunities for parents to understand a little more about what their child is learning in the school.

Schools could also invite the community into its premises and give it a role in the curricular processes. Parents or community members could come into the school as resource persons to share their knowledge and experiences in relation to a particular idea of topic being studied. For example, on the lesson on machines, the local mechanic could talk about sharing his experiences on repairing and also talk about how he learnt to repair vehicles. Similarly, while helping children to use their home language and transit to the school language, teachers may seek inputs from local language speakers to facilitate communication in mother tongues, teaching of languages and creating materials. The choice would depend upon on the particular curricular plan and the kinds of expertise that is available and accessible. The school must explore opportunities for active engagement from parents and the community in the process of learning. This relationship will help in sharing the content and pedagogy of institutionalized learning.

Overall, in order to make the school environment supportive of children, and to strengthen the relationship of the school with parents and local community, there are institutionalized structures such as parent-teacher association, local level committees and in some schools, there are strong alumni associations. During the celebration of national festivals and other events such as cultural day and sports day, most schools invite parents to come in and participate. By inviting the alumni and local residents also to the school, its importance as a community site can increase. Community involvement can also be sought for maintaining the school and its facilities. There are examples of local contributions for building school boundary walls, augmenting facilities and so on. However community participation must not mean economic burdening of poor families. On the other hand there can be an understanding that school space can be shared with the community for local events and there will be some collective responsibility in maintaining its premises.

All schools need to look for ways in which parental participation and involvement can be encouraged and sustained. Many schools do not treat parent's questions and concerns regarding the activities of the school as valid questions. Frequently private schools turn parents into mere consumers and ask them to take away their wards if they do not like something that the school is doing. Others treat poor parents as not having any legitimate stand when they come to make enquiries about their wards. Both types of treatments are disrespectful of parents and their legitimate concern for their children. Report cards that are sent home could be so designed that they give parents a clear idea of what their children have learnt, how he or she is faring and what specific things they can do to assist, instead of simply reporting marks achieved and providing a rank.

4.6 CURRICULUM SITES AND LEARNING RESOURCES

4.6.1 Texts and Books

Popular perception treats the textbook as the prime site for curriculum designing. Though curriculum planning is a much wider process, curriculum reform seldom goes beyond changing the textbook. **Improved textbooks**– carefully written and designed, professionally edited and tested, offering not merely factual information but also interactive spaces for children are important. But curricular reform can go much farther if textbooks are accompanied by several other kinds of materials. Subject **dictionaries,** for instance, can relieve the main textbook from becoming encyclopaedic, burdened by carrying definitions of technical terms, and instead allow the teacher to focus on understanding concepts. The triangular relationship between high-speed classroom teaching, heavy homework and private tuition which is a major source of stress, can be weakened if textbook writers focus on elaboration of concepts, activities, spaces to wonder about problems, exercises encouraging reflective thinking and small-group work, leaving the definition of technical terms to a subject dictionary.

Supplementary books, workbooks, and extra reading come next. In certain subjects, such as languages, the importance of such material needs no fresh recognition but the concept of such material does call for fresh thinking. Current books contain uninteresting texts in different genres, and workbooks simply repeat exercises of the types already found in textbooks. In mathematics, and natural and social sciences, such supplementary materials still need to be developed. Such books could draw children's attention away from the text to the world around them. Indeed, for subjects like art, workbooks may form the main classroom material. There are fine examples of such materials produced for the study of environment, introducing children to observing trees, birds and the natural habitat. Such resources need to become available to the teacher and for use in the classroom.

Atlases has a similar role to play in enriching the child's awareness of the earth, both as a natural and as a human habitat. Atlases of stars, flora and fauna, people and life patterns, history and culture, etc. can greatly enlarge the scope of geography, history and economics at all levels. Posters on these areas of knowledge, as well as other matters of concern on which general awareness needs to be promoted can also enhance learning. Some of these concerns include gender bias, inclusion of children with special needs, and constitutional values. Such material could be available in a resource library and the cluster level to be borrowed by schools for use, or they could be placed in the school library, or made by teachers.

Manuals and resources for teachers are just as important as textbooks. Any move to introduce a new set of textbooks or *a new kind of* textbooks should include the preparation of handbooks for teachers. These handbooks should reach principals and teachers *before* the new textbooks do. Teachers handbooks can be designed in many different ways. They need not cover the content of the textbook chapter-wise though that can be one of the approaches. Other formats can be equally valid: offering a critique of established methods and suggesting new ones, and including lists of resource materials, audios and videos, sites on the internet. These would provide tips to teachers which they could use for planning. Such source books need to be available during inservice training of teachers and during meetings when they plan their teaching units.

4.6.2 Libraries

School libraries have been a subject of policy recommendations for a long time, but a functioning library in the school continues to be a rarity. It is important that future planning treats the library as an essential component of the school at all levels. Both teachers and children need to be motivated and trained to use the library as a resource for learning, pleasure, and concentration. The school library should be conceptualized as an intellectual space where teachers, children and members of the community can expect to find the means to deepen their knowledge and imagination. A system of cataloguing books and other material available in the library needs to be developed so that children can become self-reliant library users. Apart from books and magazines, a school library should provide access to the new information technology to enable children and teachers to connect with wider world. In the initial stages of planning, block-level or cluster-level libraries can be mooted and enriched. In future India must move towards equipping every school, irrespective of its level, with a library. In many parts of the country, community libraries are functioning in rural areas and government libraries exist in many district headquarters. Futuristic planning would require amalgamation of such structures in a school library network in order to maximize the use of resources. The Raja Ram Mohan Roy Library Foundation can be given additional resources to act as a nodal agency for conceptualizing a library network for schools and to monitor it after it has been created.

In the day-to-day life of a school, the library can serve many different kinds of purposes. Restricting use of the library to one period a week seldom allows children to cultivate a taste for reading. Facilities are to be provided to allow children to borrow books. Training of teachers in library management and use is required to overcome this situation. Where the size of the school building permits a separate room for the library, it is important to pay attention to creating a positive ethos in this space by providing good lighting and seating arrangements. It should even be possible for a teacher to conduct a class in the library; drawing upon its resources for it could also serve as a place for holding discussions, watching a craftsman from the community giving a demonstration or to listen to a storyteller. Creating such resource libraries to support teachers, at the cluster and block levels will complement and strengthen curriculum renewal. Each block could specialize in a subject area so that together there are adequate resources in the district.

4.6.3 Education Technology

The significance of **Educational Technology (ET)** as a site for curriculum planning has been widely recognized, but detailed guidance and strategies for its educationally optimum use have not yet been worked out. Generally, technology has been used as a medium to disseminate, and as a way of addressing the scarcity of good teachers—usually the consequence of poor recruitment policies. ET which is used to redress the problem of quality of teaching can only exacerbate the disillusionment of teachers with teaching. If ET is to become a means of enhancing curricular reform, it must treat the majority of teachers and children not merely as consumers but as active producers. There must be widespread consultation regarding use and during development and implementation. ET facilities need to be used at all level-schools, cluster and block resource centres, district, state and the national level-in order to provide *hands on experience* of using ET. Such experiences, provided to children, teachers and teacher educators, could include something as simple as audio-recording of an interview with a village elder, to making a video film or a video game. Providing children more direct access to multi-media equipment and Information Communication Technology (ICT), and allowing them to mix and make their own productions and to present their own experiences could provide them with new opportunities to explore their own creative imaginations.

Such an experience of ET production, rather than only watching and listening to programmes, can lay the foundation for far better utilisation of the country's enormous ET facilities. Interactive, net enabled computers, rather than only CDbased computer usage would facilitate a meaningful integration of computers, and enhance school curriculum in rural and remote areas by increasing connectivity and access to ideas, and information. It is such two-way interactivity, rather than one-way reception that would make technology educational.

Rather than trying to reproduce and mimic classroom situations, or teach the textbook content, or animate lab experiments, ET could realize far better potential if topics are taken but developed into non-didactic explorations, leaving learners free to relate to the knowledge web progressively, and learn at their levels of interest. Such access to knowledge in regional languages is still very limited, and is one of the main reasons for the persisting and growing divide in learners from urban and rural schools and learners from regional language vs. English medium schools. The potential of such encyclopaedia and documentaries for children is still under-developed. Materials such as textbooks, workbooks or handbooks for teachers can be designed with the awareness of existing stocks of good-quality audio or video material and sites where extra resources are available on the net. Classics of cinema need to be made accessible through such measures. For instance, a child studying about village life should have easy access to Satyajit Ray's classic, *Pather Panchali,* either as a CD to be borrowed from the CRC or to be viewed on a nationally managed website. Future textbooks need to be conceptualized and designed in ways that might integrate knowledge in different subjects and experiences facilitating the assimilation of knowledge. For instance, a middle school textbook which discusses the history of Rajasthan and mentions Meera should be able to offer the text of a *bhajan* composed by her, and also refer to a source where that *bhajan* has been archived, so that children can listen to MS Subbulakshmi singing it.

Integration of knowledge and experience along these lines would take away the sense of burden and boredom which our present-day education induces. In science and mathematics, and in teaching children with disabilities, the potential of ET, including IT, is widely appreciated. It is important to realize this potential to achieve curricular goals, with more age-specific planning on use of ET. Governments and other agencies responsible for financial planning need to take this fuller range of ET's demands and benefits.

4.6.4 Tools and Laboratories

Equipping the school with tools which are necessary for art and craft work is an imperative. These curricular areas can contribute to achieving the aim of making the school space a creative space, only if we can mindfully plan for resources. The heritage crafts require, in their weekly or fortnightly cycles of routine, tools and instruments such as looms, lathes, scissors and embroidery frames, depending on the craft. It is important not to let this sector of curricular planning suffer from gender or caste bias, or else one of its key promises will be lost: namely, the promise of promoting a culture of active engagement with one's material and human environment with imagination and cooperation. The same is true of the arts, which in addition to being integrated into other curricular areas would also need specialized materials and tools. The opportunity to handle tools and acquire dexterity in using them, and also learning to take care of and maintain them are invaluable experiences for all children, and their special cognitive significance for children with special needs is well recognized. Investment in training of the child's senses and faculties with the help of art plays a vital role in strengthening literacy, and developing a culture of peace.

Schools, particularly in rural areas are poorly equipped with science labs, or equipment for mathematical activities. The absence of such facilities drastically narrows subject options for children denying them equal opportunities for learning and future life chances. It is hence important that resources are made available for laboratories with adequate facilities in schools. While elementary school can benefit from a science and mathematics corner, secondary and higher secondary schools require well-equipped laboratories.

4.6.5 Other Sites and Spaces

Sites of curriculum which are physically located outside the school premises are just as important as the ones discussed so far. These are sites like local monuments and museums, natural phenomena such as rivers and hills, everyday spaces such as market places and post office. The teacher's ability to plan the school schedule in a manner that permits imaginative use of such resources directly affects the quality of education children might receive at a school. Restriction of classroom activities to what is written in the textbook implies a serious impediment to the growth of children's interests and capabilities. Quite a few such impediments result from the rigid observation of the school's daily or annual routine. The night sky is not available for the study of stars simply because the school does not open its gates or give access to its roof at night. Watching the setting sun or observing the arrival of monsoon in June fall outside the school's timetable. Exchange visits between schools in different parts of the country, and even the neighbouring SAARC countries could become important ways of promoting mutual understanding.

Teachers and educational administrators would have to join hands to release the system from such rigidities. In addition, syllabus makers and the writers of textbooks and teachers handbooks would also have to get into the details of the planning of learning activities which would widen the scope of the curriculum. This would require breaking away from the mindset that excursions, and activities related to art and craft are 'extracurricular'.

4.6.6 Need for Plurality and Alternative Materials

The pluralistic and diverse nature of Indian society definitely makes a strong case for preparing a variety of not only textbooks but other materials, so as to promote children's creativity, participation and interest, thereby enhancing their learning. No one textbook can cater to the diverse needs of different groups of students. Further the same content/concept can be taught in different ways. Schools, government or private, could have the choice of textbooks to follow for different subjects. Boards or textbook bureaus could consider developing more than one series of books, or even endorsing books published by other publishers and allowing schools to choose from a range. As far back as 1953, the Report of the Secondary Education Commission made a number of recommendations to remove the defects in textbooks, wherein it was pointed out that: "No single textbook should be prescribed for any subject of study, but a reasonable number of books which satisfy the standards laid down should be recommended, leaving the choice to the school concerned". In its section on the Essentials for Curricula Development, the Kothari Commission Report emphasized that the curricular revision had been of an ad-hoc character and that the curriculum is prepared at the state level and prescribed uniformly for all schools. Such procedures undermine the agency of teachers and head teachers, and render the spirit of exploration and innovation impossible. The Report categorically stated that basic to the success of any attempt at curriculum improvement is the preparation of suitable textbooks, teachers guides and other kinds of learning resources.

4.6.7 Organising and Pooling Resources

Teaching aids and other materials, as well as books, toys and games help make schools interesting for children. In some states of the country, good use has been made of the funding assistance through DPEP and other programmes to acquire and develop teaching learning materials. A lot of ready-made materials do exists, and teachers, cluster and block level resource persons need to become better acquainted with the range of materials available and how to use them. There are also many new kinds of printed materials for teachers and children being produced by NGO groups and small entrepreneurs. In addition there are locally available materials that cost little but which are very useful to be kept in a classroom, especially in the primary school grade. Teachers need to explore various types of raw materials that can be used to make teaching aids that will last year after year, so that the precious time they invest in making these things is put to good use. Styro-foam and card board are neither strong enough nor attractive—other materials such as rexine, rubber, and cloth are interesting alternatives.

Other kinds of resource materials, such as maps and picture folders, and specific equipments could be shared between schools if they are placed in the **cluster centre** which then can serve as a **resource library** so that for the period of teaching the teacher borrows materials from the cluster and subsequently returns them to the cluster to enable some other teachers to borrow. In this way resources gathered by one teacher can also be utilized by others, and it would become possible to have multiple sets necessary for the whole class to use.

The availability of such resources depends on the funds available and many schools are poorly provided. How can the school build such resources? Some government programmes, for instance, Operation Blackboard, has laid down norms for the minimum materials that should be available in each primary and upper primary school. Similarly, there are new schemes that allow for cycles and toys to be purchased for a cluster of schools. Schools could benefit from these opportunities, and also explore the possibilities that are available at the local level to augment its teaching-learning and play material. There is growing emphasis on educational technology for 'effective' learning. Some schools are now being equipped with computers, and in some areas radio and TV based instruction is being introduced.

Ultimately the use of such materials requires planning if it is to be effective and become a part of the overall plan to enhance participation and understanding. Teachers would need to prepare and plan if the materials she introduces into the room are for the purpose of demonstration. If an activity is being planned, then there must be enough sets for everyone in the class to use, individually or in small groups. If only one child is able to handle materials while all others watch, it is a waste of learning time.

Labs have always been talked about as a part of the science teaching in middle and high school. Yet these are still not available on the scale required. As a part of the effort to provide all children with necessary hands on experience of equipments and experiments given in their science curriculum, at least at the cluster level, the resource centre may serve as a cluster-lab. Schools in the cluster could plan their time table so that for half a day, once a week, their science lab class is held at the cluster level lab. Craft labs too could be developed at least at the cluster of block levels in order to facilitate access to better equipments.

In engendering a culture of learning, not only the classroom, but the space of the school itself and the world outside the school could become the landscape in which a range of activities are organized. Teachers can devise activities, projects and studies, both drawing from textbooks and going beyond the textbooks to encourage children to explore, investigate and construct knowledge.

4.7 TIME

Earlier documents have all included a section of recommendations on instructional time. Important concerns which we endorse from earlier documents include the need for the system to ensure that the **total number of instructional days are not compromised**, and the total number of days for the curriculum should be 200 days as recommended in NCF-1988. The proposal made in the 1988 NCF on the relative allocation of time for different broad curricular areas can be taken as a broad guideline. Within this we suggest ways in which we can work out possibilities and methods to enrich the total time spent by each child in school from the point of view of learning.

The **school annual calendar** is currently decided at the State level. There have been several suggestions made in the past also, that the annual calendar could be planned at a more decentralized level, so that it is closer to the calendar of local activities and weather. The plan for such calendars could be decentralized to the district level and decided in consultation with the zilla panchayats.

Considerations for making the changes could be the weather conditions. For example, where monsoon is very heavy and areas are prone to flood, it is better for schools to remain closed and have a vacation period at that time. Parents in some areas ask schools to function during summer months also as it is too hot to go out even to play. There are also areas where parents would prefer that the vacation comes at the time of harvest so that children participate in the family occupation. Such adjustments would permit children to learn from the world they live in by acquiring important life-skills and attitudes, instead of forgoing their lives in the local community and becoming alienated from it for the sake of school. Local holidays could be decided at the block level. The scheduling of various school events would need to be planned by all school faculty together, along with inputs from the village/school education committee. Thematic learning across the school grades or excursions would also need to be planned in advance.

Needless to say, we need to safeguard against the misuse of such flexibility. Not all communities are benign spaces for children. It would go against the educational aims of the school if the community takes advantage of such flexibility to perpetuate cultural practices that are discriminatory or stereotype children on the lines of gender, religion or caste. It also could lend itself to children getting drawn into child labour. Children have a right to leisure and to play, and have time for themselves. Some local traditions and cultures are supportive of such a childhood, others less so. Often girls are burdened from an early age, with domestic chores. Increasingly children are under great pressure to study and are placed in tuition classes before and after school, and they get little time to play. Schools must engage with children's families and their communities in a continuous dialogue to argue for and protect these rights of children.

The **timings of the school day** could be decided at each school level, in consultation with the gram panchayat, keeping in mind issues such as how far children need to travel to get to school. This flexibility is suggested only in order to facilitate children's participation in school. While saying this, we strongly maintain that the time spent in school itself, and on learning in the school, cannot be in any way compromised or reduced below six hours a day (and 3 hours for the ECCE period). Where teachers and children travel to school from a far off place, it would befit the overall societal concern for children if bus timings are changed to enable teachers and students to reach the school and leave at convenient time, instead of compelling them to routinely come late and leave early.

The school day, week, month, term and year, need to be planned for as a **mixture of routine and variation**, as children need a little of both, and the kinds of learning we would like them to experience have different requirements. We share some organizational ideas that could form the basis for planning and enriching children's time spent in school, and also some aspects which relate to institutional arrangements for the same.

In most schools the day begins with a **morning assembly**. There are many schools that utilize this time where the entire school gathers to do things together. While reading the headlines of the morning newspaper, performing some exercises and singing the national anthem are some common activities, other could also be added: for example, singing together, or listening to a story, or inviting a person from the local community or an outside guest to speak to the children, or small events to mark some significant local or national happening. Classes that have undertaken some interesting projects could also use this time to share their work with the whole school. If not everyday, such longer morning assemblies could be planned once or twice a week. In composite schools, depending on the theme, junior-school assembly and senior school assembly could be held separately. News head lines that are significant, for example the bus journey to Muzzafarabad, could provide a theme for a special session on that day, and get woven into the curriculum.

In most documents a **period** has been presented as a basic unit of 45minutes of teaching-learning in the timetable. Frequently, however, this is compromised into 30 to 35 minutes, which cannot constitue a meaningful length to engage with learning. A period can, in general, serve as an organizational unit for many text based lessons.

But there is need for the school timetable to allow for other kinds of longer periods lasting an hour, or one-andhalf hours (a double period), for other kinds of such as craft or art work, activities, projects, or lab work. Such lengths of time are also essential to undertake crosssubject integrated learning, and for effective group work. Needless to say, in a multigrade class situation, the teacher needs a more flexible way to plan for children's learning time in sessions which are teacher-led, those which are self-directed, those in which two or more grades could be combined, etc. While certain subject areas such as language and mathematics need learning time everyday, others do not. The weekly timetable could involve variation from but, balanced over the week. What is essential is to be able to take stock of time spent in learning different subject areas and to introduce corrections if the teachers find that more or less time is being spent or needed, on what is being spent.

4.8 TEACHER'S AUTONOMY AND PROFESSIONAL INDEPENDENCE

Teacher autonomy is essential to ensure a learning environment that addresses children's diverse needs. As much as the learner requires space freedom, flexibility, and respect, the teacher also requires the same. Currently the system of administrative hierarchies and control, examinations, and centralized planning for curriculum reform, all constrain the autonomy of the headmaster and teacher. Even when there is curricular freedom, teachers do not feel confident that they can exercise it without being taken to task by the administration for doing things differently. It is therefore essential to enable and support them to exercise choices. As much as the classroom needs to nurture a democratic, flexible and accepting culture, so also the school institution and the bureaucratic structure need to do the same. Not only should the teacher receive orders and information, but equally the voice of the teacher should be heard by those higher up, often taking decisions that affect the immediate classroom life and culture in the school. Relationships between teachers and their heads and principals must be informed by equality and mutual respect, and decision making must be on the basis of dialogue and discussion. The annual, monthly and weekly calendar of activities need to provide time for such staff interactions to review and plan. There is need to encourage an atmosphere that facilitates collaborative efforts between teachers. There must also be mechanisms for conflict resolution.

Often technologies such as radio and TV are introduced into their classrooms without consulting teachers on whether they would like to have it and what they would like it to do for them. Once it is there in the classroom, they are expected to use it, when they have no control over what it will deliver, or how it will integrate with their own teaching plans.

4.8.1 Time for Reflection and Planning

- On a daily basis (at least 45 minutes) to review the day, make notes on children to follow up the next day, and organize materials for the next days' lessons, (this is in addition to time which they may need to correct homework).
- On a weekly basis (at least two/three hours) to take stock of learning, to work out details of activities and projects proposed, and to plan a group of lessons (unit) for the coming week.
- On a monthly/term basis (minimum of one day) to review their work, children's learning and map the contours of the learning activities planned for the groups they teach.
- At the beginning and end of the year (two or three days each) to evolve an annual plan for the school, in which they locate activities that would involve the whole school, such as local holidays that need to be provided, annual events (national events, sports days, cultural events), days for parent-teacher meetings. They would also plan excursions and field trips for their class-groups, and for any projects that two or more classes would do

together. They would also be involved in activities of preparing the school and class environment, putting up and changing posters and displays, organizing children's work, etc. Such planning time is also essential for the school to review its relationship with the community and identify points of focused action in the year such as enrollment, retention, school attendance and school achievement.

- Current in-service training related time allocation (compulsory 20 days per year) could be partly diverted towards making time available for such review, reflection and planning).
- Monthly meetings organized for teachers at the cluster level could be based on groups of teachers teaching similar subjects and grade levels, so that they can share ideas and plan teaching for the forthcoming month together.

OBSERVATIONS

This chapter highlights the need for providing minimum infrastructure and material facilities. The most important point to be noted is its emphasis that teacher-pupil ratio higher than 1.30 is not desirable at any stage of education. In fact this is the very vital issue which plays an important role in assuring quality education. All programmes of reform revolve round this. But then where are funds for carrying out this suggestion? The report is silent on this aspect.

Common Schooling—The document emphasises that this ideal put forward by the Kothari Commission four decades age is all the more relevant. But the question is! Who will ensure this!

Textbooks and Books—On the one hand the document talks about lessening the school bag and on the other hand favours dictionaries, supplementary books, work books and extra-reading material besides improved textbooks.

Allocation of Time—The NCF refers to the 1988 NCF regarding allocation of time. The 1988 NCF observed, "After taking into account the member of days required for holding terminal examinations, school functions, etc. at least 200 days in a year should be available for effective instruction. An early child education centre should function for three hours a day. A primary school should function for five years a day out of which four hours should be available for instructional work. For the upper primary and secondary schools, the duration of a school should be six hours, out of which five hours should be kept for instructional work, and the rest utilised for morning assembly. The duration of a class period should be around 40 minutes."

Suggestive Time for Different Curricular Areas

Stage and Subjects	*Percentage of Time*
Primary Stage (5 years)	
Language/Languages	30%
Mathematics	15%
Environmental Studies	15%
Work Experience	20%
Art Education	10%
Health and Physical Education	10%
Total	**100%**
Upper Primary Stage (3 years)	
Language/Languages	32%
Mathematics	12%
Science	12%
Social Sciences	12%
Work Experience	12%
Art Education	10%
Health and Physical Education	10%
Total	**100%**
Secondary Stage (2 years)	
Language/Languages	30%
Mathematics	13%
Science	13%
Social Sciences	13%
Work Experience	13%
Art Education	8%
Health and Physical Education	10%
Total	**100%**

Teacher's Autonomy and Professional Independence

The document considers teacher autonomy very essential to ensure a learning experience that addresses children's needs. It is doubtful that this recommendation would carry the day. In the existing situation, it appears to be a 'utopian' concept. Who would like to part with power?

6

Systemic Reforms and Epilogue

The chapter heading of chapter 5 of the draft is Systematic Reforms followed by Epilogue which are discussed in the subsequent pages.

The dimensions of the national framework for school curriculum that have been outlined in the preceding chapters are derived from related aims of education with a social conscience, focusing on learners who are actively engaged with constructing rather than only receiving knowledge through their individual and collective endeavours. Such a curricular vision needs to be supported and sustained with systemic reforms of structures and institutions that nurture practices supportive of children's inclusion in school and their learning. Important among these is, firstly, the system for preparing teachers and supporting their professional practices through monitoring and academic leadership; secondly, the system for producing textbooks and learning materials; thirdly, decentralization and panchayati raj institutions, and finally perhaps the single most important structural feature—the examination system. The curriculum is realized in the activities planned for by the teachers and experienced by the children. The school ethos and practice of teachers depend critically on the architecture of the system. What critical areas that require attention are identified and discussed hereafter

5.1 CONCERN FOR QUALITY

Curriculum reforms are at the heart of any wide-ranging initiative that may be taken to improve the quality of educational provision at different stages. The prevailing curricular reality needs to be addressed in the following terms:

- The tendency to confuse knowledge with information must be curbed. This tendency encourages the transfer of topics from higher to lower levels.

- Treatment of children's learning as an isolated outcome should be replaced by the application of developmental norms which assume a holistic pattern of growth in motivation and capacity.
- Curricular choices have to be made with due regard to the child's context, ensuring flexibility and diversity of approaches emphasized in the NPE, 1986, and POA, 1992.
- Professionalisation of teaching, along the lines recommended by the Chattopodhyaya Commission, 1984, should be reflected in policies governing recruitment, preservice, and in-service training, and working conditions.
- Educational technology should be viewed as a supplement rather than as a substitute for hands-on experience, both for classroom teaching and for teacher-training.

These recommendations should suffice to indicate our primary concern, that quality is a systemic attribute rather than only a feature of instruction or attainment. As an over-arching characteristic, quality expresses the system's capacity to reform itself for enhancing its ability to remedy its own weaknesses and to develop new capabilities. The key reforms required in our system today and those which will enable it to overcome its internal rigidity and its indifference to changing circumstances. This challenge is identical to what the POA, 1992 had stressed in the need to modernize for greater flexibility. For curricular and training practices to remain relevant in a decentralized system, it is necessary to articulate the objectives and methods of reform with clarity and precision. The following deserve priority:

- Equipping the school for taking decisions at its own level in areas such as purchase of material, collaboration with local institutions and, involving other schools in the area including the private schools.
- Linkages between primary, upper primary and secondary levels in the processes of syllabus-designing and textbook preparation.
- Setting up of structures which enable school teachers and subject experts drawn from institutions of higher learning to work together for syllabus and textbook revision.
- Creation of spaces where local level representative institutions can work closely with teachers to enhance efficiency.
- Cooperation between decision-making bodies and NGOs.
- Encouraging greater communication and transparency between different structures and levels of decision making.

Quality is not merely a measure of efficiency; it also has a value dimension. The attempt to improve the quality of education will succeed only if it goes hand in hand with steps to promote social justice. As an objective of curriculum planning, social justice has many obvious implications, but there are some subtle implications as well. One obvious implication is that special efforts will be required to ensure that education promotes an inclusive identity. Children belonging to religious and linguistic minorities need special provision and care in accordance with the perspective reflected in the Constitution. In the case of tribal languages, certain states have taken appreciative measures to facilitate early schooling in the child's home language. A more adequate set of measures, providing for multi-lingual facility on the part of the teacher, is needed. Similarly, policy measures taken to widen the curricular scope of *madrassa* education need to be strengthened.

The subtler implications of social justice as an objective of curriculum policy are more challenging. These relate to teacher awareness and capacities, flexibility and imaginative coordination among syllabus designers, textbook writers and teachers.

For education to remain a nurturing experience for all children, irrespective of their socio-economic and cultural background, concrete steps are needed in teacher-education, curriculum, and in the procedures used for syllabus and textbook preparation. Teacher-education programmes, like B.Ed and M.Ed in place today, pay inadequate attention to the responsibility a teacher has in constructing a classroom culture which might provide an inclusive environment to children especially girls from oppressed or marginalized social backgrounds. In syllabus designing and textbook writing, the items showing sensitivity to culture differences often come in as afterthoughts rather than as in-built features of the process. The case of gender and special needs is similar. One of the numerous messages received by NCERT in the course of deliberations over the national curriculum framework review came from a teenage girl who suggested that specific measures are needed to inculcate greater self-awareness among boys regarding their behaviour towards girls. Such an idea could be extended to cover all aspects of a culturally inclusive classroom and school policy.

5.1.1 Academic Planning and Monitoring for Quality

The current practice of academic planning for school education is largely a 'top down' annual exercise. Its focus is on how teaching time should be allocated for teaching of subject content over the year, and stipulating other activities that will be conducted in schools. Typically this is done by SCERTs or the Directorates/Departments of education, and presecribed uniformly for all schools in the state. The importance of

school level planning was emphasised by the Kothari Commission when it underscored the need for each school to prepare an 'institutional plan' and evolve a 'development programme spread over a period of time'.

To be meaningful academic planning has to be done in a participative manner by heads and teachers. One component of planning will include augmentation and improvement of physical resources of the school. The second is to address the diverse needs of students and to identify the inputs and academic support that the school needs in order to respond to these needs. The planning exercise is an important process through which schools can enlist the involvement and support of the larger community in the education of the children. This includes the village education committees and other statutory bodies. Micro planning, which includes village level mapping of school participation (non-enrolled children, attendance patterns, children with special needs, etc.) as well as identification of human resources allows the school to plan on a more realistic basis for every child. In order for more independence at the school level both at the stage of planning and to attain greater implementation, it is necessary that financial allocations permit greater flexibility regarding schemes and norms and also greater transparency and accountability of budget allocations and expenditure.

There is need to prepare the system to engage in more extensive genuine planning from below, rather than only applying the arithmetic of unit costs for programmes determined at the State or National centres. Only then can 'autonomy' and 'choice' of schools and teachers, as well as responsibility of the schools towards the needs of children become substantive. A broad framework for planning upwards, beginning with schools identifying focus areas, with subsequent consolidation at the cluster and block could create a genuinely decentralized district level planning. Setting targets, planning for and being responsible for them would then become feasible at all these levels.

5.1.2 Academic Leadership in Schools and for School Monitoring

The potential role of Headmasters in providing academic leadership to their schools is yet to be adequately realized. At present they are seen largely as the administrative authority within the school, though they lack the necessary control to exercise this authority, or even to ensure regular school functioning. Often they are equipped with neither the capacity nor authority to exercise choice and judgment relating to school curriculum. Headmasters (and teachers) need to be able to identify specific supports they require for their schools, articulate their expectations regarding the content of trainings and school visits from the cluster and block personnel and participate in the process of monitoring and supervision. Currently they are not differentiated enough from teachers with regards to their academic roles. The role that the headmasters, and indeed the community of headmasters can play, within a cluster of schools must be highlighted. Capacity building for this must receive attention.

Schools are now the focus of an increasing number of programmes to enhance quality, spread awareness about societal concerns relating to the environment, health and so on. Headmasters are often besieged by the numerous programmes they are called upon to conduct and participate. Programmes often lack clarity regarding their objectives and methodology and their activities tend to overlap. It is important that as part of the process of school level planning, they should be able to participate in decisions about programmes they need and how they should be integrated into regular school activities. These programmes could then be coordinated at the cluster and block level.

Conventionally, monitoring of schools has been through the Inspectorate system. This system has served largely to exercise authority and control rather than provide academic support to teachers. The school Inspectors perform a number of functions, one of which one is to visit schools under their purview. Their visits are usually few and far between, during which the students and teachers tend to present positive picture of the school, regardless of ground realities, due to fear of punishment. This reduces monitoring to a 'policing' function. Monitoring for quality must be seen as a process that enables and provides constructive feedback in relation to the teaching and learning processes within specific classroom contexts. The monitoring system put in place must be carefully analysed in relation to its objectives, and the norms and practices that are to be institutionalized to achieve the objectives. It must provide for sustained interaction with individual schools in terms of teachinglearning processes within the classroom context.

5.1.3 The Panchayats and Education

The 73rd Constitutional Amendment established the 3-tier panchayat raj system in the country with elected bodies at gram, taluk and zilla levels to enable people to think, decide and act for their collective interest, to provide for greater participation of the people in development, to ensure more effective implementation of rural development programmes in the state, and to plan and implement programmes for economic development and social justice. The 73rd Constitutional amendment identified 29 subjects for transfer to the panchayats, including primary and secondary education, adult and non-formal education, libraries, technical training and vocational education. All State governments enacted their State

Panchayat Raj Acts in order to realize the Constitutional mandate of decentralized democracy and development.

Overlaps and Ambiguities in Functions

Several States in the country have identified functions and activities for implementation at different tiers of panchayat raj functioning. In several states a vast gamut of functions is assigned to PRIs at every level. In practice however, PRIs especially Taluk and Gram Panchayats, discharge few tasks. Barring disbursement of salaries in some states, Taluk and Gram panchayats discharge practically no functions of any significance in the sectors of Education, Health, Women and Child Development and Social Welfare. Moreover, there are huge ambiguities and overlaps in the functions and tasks to be discharged at different levels. These ambiguities often results in conflicts between the three tiers especially with respect to: Who plans? Who decides? Who selects? Who accords approval? Who implements? Who releases funds? Who monitors? Indeed there is no role clarity between functions at different levels.

Principle of Subsidiarity: The principle of subsidiarity is the bedrock of panchayat raj. The principle of subsidiarity stipulates: 'What can be done best at a particular level should be done at that level and not at higher levels. All that can be done optimally at the lowest level should be done at that level.' This necessitates a rational and realistic analysis of the functions that require to be discharged at different levels of panchayat raj institutions, devolution of those functions to those levels of panchayat raj, simultaneously ensuring that required funds are devolved to that level to discharge that function and transact the activity.

Strengthening Panchayat Raj: The practice of setting up parallel bodies in the form of *autonomous registered bodies*, for example, Zilla Saksharta Samities, DPEP Societies, SSA Societies at the State level, and similar bodies at the taluk and village level, has severely undermined the powers of panchayat raj institutions. These parallel bodies have sprouted in large numbers across different sectors. Each village has them – there are village education committees, watershed committees, ryot mitra committees, forest committees, water users associations, none of which are answerable to panchayats. These committees receive large funds from external donor agencies, and are dominated largely by the village elite.

In short the major problems in Panchayat Raj functioning are that there is:

- No one-to-one co-relation between functions assigned to the different tiers of panchayat raj and funds devolved.

- Tendency to form parallel committees at village level marginalise democratically elected bodies These committees undermine the stature of democratically elected bodies and make a mockery of peoples' participation in local planning.

Over the recent past, there has been a growing emphasis on maintaining a large data base at the block/district level on indicators such as enrolment, drop-out, achievement etc. These are also used as yardsticks to monitor schools and for larger school management. While official insistence on regular maintaining of detailed records in relation to these indicators has burdened the school, it has also led to a unnecessary emphasis on quantitative indices of school performance (often leading to data of questionable quality) at various levels without adequate stops to link academic planning and the process of curriculum transaction.

Block Resource Centres (BRC) and the Cluster Resource Centres (CRC) are now present in almost all districts to monitor schools and teachers through follow up. In order to provide training, DIETs have been set up at the district level. Lack of role clarity and overlap of activities afflict the functioning of these organisations. Quite often, personnel in resource centers are mostly reduced to administrative and data collection functionaries. Given the perspective of decentralized school level academic planning, and the active and creative involvement of teachers in defining the nature of curriculum transaction to address the needs of children, it is urgent that the BRCs and CRCs are energized so that they play a facilitating role. It would be necessary to define the roles of resource persons in these centres, build their capacities by deepening their subject knowledge and training competence, and to provide them space to function with some autonomy. Rather than routinely conducting workshops designed elsewhere, these centres could focus on conducting workshops along with followup, based on needs they locally identify. Norms for schools visits, guidelines for systematic monitoring, feed back and academic support will also have to be evolved. There is also need for institutional mechanisms that co-ordinate and build upon the work done by resource centers at different levels in order that synergies emerge.

In order to strengthen school-based academic support for teachers, it is necessary to identify and create a pool of resource persons at the level of the village, cluster and block, and similarly in urban areas that can contribute to regular inputs that teachers require, provide support to new ideas and practices and help work them through. It should be possible to institutionalize such support at the level of the cluster/block, which can then be integrated into a regular teachersupport programme and funds should be made available for it.

5.2 TEACHER EDUCATION FOR CURRICULUM RENEWAL

Though the professional preparation of teachers has been recognized as crucially important since the 1960s, ground reality remains a matter of great concern. The Kothari Commission (1964-66) emphasized the need for teacher education to be brought into mainstream academic life, but teacher education Institutes continue to exist as insular organizations. The Chattopadhyaya Committee (1983-85) recommended that the length of training for a Secondary teacher be five years following completion of class 12; it also suggested that colleges of science and arts introduce an Education Department to allow students to opt for teacher education. The Yashpal Committee Report (1993), *Learning without Burden*, noted; "The emphasis in these programmes should be on enabling trainees to acquire the ability for self-learning and independent thinking."

In reality, however, teacher education programmes today train teachers to adjust to the needs of a system in which education is seen as the transmission of information. Attempts at curricular reform have not been adequately supported with efforts at teacher education. Large-scale recruitment of para-teachers has diluted the identity of teachers as professionals. Most initiatives of the 1990's focused on in-service training of teachers. This has accentuated the divide between pre-service and in-service teacher education. School teachers continue to be isolated from centres of higher learning, and their real needs remain unaddressed. Existing programmes do not address curriculum design and issues of relations between school and society. There is little engagement with the numerous recent innovative educational experiments.

5.2.1 Developing the Professional Identity of the Teacher

A vital first step is to reaffirm faith in the central role of the teacher and in the importance of quality pre-service education. Professional training of teachers needs to be linked to post-graduate studies in different subjects in order to promote interdisciplinary enquiry. Possible mechanisms for this are provisions for integrated undergraduate studies in teacher education, and the study of education as an elective subject at undergraduate and postgraduate levels. The B. El. Ed. programme of elementary teacher education provides an example of such an opening. One way of breaking the insularity of teacher education programmes would be to locate programmes of teacher education within colleges of general education; another would be designing postgraduate programmes in education in a manner that allows students to choose course credits across different disciplines. This may also help identify relevant questions for research and reflective inquiry.

5.2.2 Critical Concerns in Design and Practice

Experience indicates that the need to enhance the language proficiency of the teacher is very real. Courses of language proficiency should form an integral part of pre-service programmes. Experience also suggests that the assumption that a few practice teaching lessons suffice for links to form between theories of child development and instructional methods of teaching specific subjects is mistaken. Teacher education programmes must make a conscious effort to design courses that generate a deeper understanding of such linkages.

In existing programmes of teacher education knowledge is treated as 'given'. Trainees are not expected to critically examine the curriculum, syllabi and textbooks; teachers are expected to adjust to existing realities. Again, it is assumed that teachers can easily set aside their own assumptions about children, knowledge and learning. However, most teacher education programmes provide little scope for trainees to reflect on their experiences and assumptions, and thus fail to empower teachers as agents of change. So, while training them to prepare meticulous lesson plans, such programmes fail to make trainees aware of underlying assumptions and the consequences of practices based on them.

The need is to create teachers who can respond to the needs of children and their learning. Pre-service programmes should be designed to engage trainee teachers with the larger context in which education is situated, engage with children in real contexts, and to critically question their own beliefs about knowledge and learning, and their positions vis-à-vis gender, caste, equity and justice. Such processes may help promote habits of independent thinking, selflearning and the capacity to adjust the system to respond to the needs of children. Teacher education programmes at present are deficient in this regard. By weaving theory with their experience and with children's social milieu, trainees are likely to develop the habit of independent thinking. Some efforts could be directed at providing opportunities for the following:

- Understanding self and others (including one's beliefs, assumptions and emotions); developing the ability for selfanalysis, self-evaluation, adaptability, flexibility, creativity and innovation, self-learning, reflection, assimilation and articulation of new ideas; for developing capacities self-directed learning and being self-critical, and for learning to working in groups.

- Observing and engaging with children, communicating with, and relating to them.
- Generating understanding, knowledge and examining disciplinary knowledge and social realities; relating subject matter with the social milieu.
- Developing skills in pedagogy, observation, documentation, analysis, drama, craft, story-telling and reflective inquiry.
- Learning how to integrate manual work with academic knowledge of different subjects.

5.2.3 Some Points of Departure

Understanding the learning child is a major priority of teacher education. The key point of departure would be understanding children by observing and interacting with them in diverse social, economic and cultural contexts. Spaces could be provided for direct observation of children, at play and at work. Assignments could be evolved to help teachers understand children's questions and observations about natural and social phenomena, to enquire into children's thinking and learning, and to learn to listen to children with attention, humour and empathy.

Learning is to be appreciated as occurring in shared social and everyday contexts. Ideas expressed by educational thinkers such as Gandhi, Tagore, Sri Aurobindo, Gijubhai, J. Krishnamurty Dewey and others are often studied in a piecemeal manner, without the necessary context and the concern these ideas emanated from. No wonder they are studied and memorized, but seldom applied by the very teacher educators who present these ideas to the trainee teachers. To make ideas come alive teacher education needs to provide spaces for **engagement with concerns of Indian society and its pluralistic nature**, and issues such as identity, gender, equity and poverty. This can help teachers evolve an understanding of the purpose of education and its relationship with society.

Conventional teacher education focuses exclusively on methodologies for teaching individual school subjects; it is assumed that trainees possess the necessary subject knowledge, which they draw upon when needed. But engagement with subject content is essential if we want teachers to present content in appropriate ways. Through observations and experiments, concepts learnt during general education in school and college can be reviewed in order to **reconstruct knowledge.** Projects in science could involve laboratory work, library reference, field surveys, group discussions, etc. to explore questions that children ask – for example *Why is the sky blue*? *Why do humans have two hands ?*

Mathematical concepts can be reconstructed through activities, using concrete materials and craft-based activities, such as weaving. Integration with the manual activity involved in work helps trainees appreciate the nature of subject knowledge, apart from generating values like dignity of work and co-operation and harmony.

A key departure is necessary in **pedagogic theory** to shift focus from pure disciplinary knowledge to the learner and her context; for example a course on language pedagogy would study the language characteristics of learners, socio-cultural aspects of language learning, and language as a process. This may mean moving away from the conventional focus on language as a subject which emphasizes structure rather than usage. To help trainees draw insights, they would need to listen to children's reading, observe and analyze reading difficulties, examine mismatches between language at school and home, analyze textbooks in terms of presentation, style and language, and so on. In mathematics, the focus could be to understand the nature of children's thinking through theory and observation, examine mathematical language, study researches on children's learning, and examine errors and mathematics phobia. In environmental education, history or geography, the study could be based on excursions, drawing on local sources of evidence – rocks, leaves, stamps, flags, reports, newspapers, documents, local maps, atlases, and so on.

Programmes should provide **internships in schools** to sustain engagement with children in school situations, and experiences of teaching children alongside regular teachers. The intern would get the opportunity to learn to set realistic goals for children's learning, curricula content and pedagogy. A sustained contact through internship would help teachers choose, design, organize and conduct meaningful classroom activities, critically reflect upon their own practices, and develop strategies for evaluating children's learning for feedback into curriculum and pedagogy.

5.2.4 In–Service Education and Training of Teachers

In-service education can play a significant role in the professional growth of teachers and as agent for change in school related practices. It helps teachers gain confidence by engaging with their practices and reaffirming their experiences. It provides opportunities to engage with other teachers professionally and to update knowledge. The Education Commission (1964-66) recommended that in-service education for teachers should be organized by universities and teacher organizations to enable every teacher to receive two or three months of in-service education once in five years; that such programmes should be based on research inputs;

that training institutions should work on a 12-month basis and organize programmes like refresher courses, seminars, workshops and summer institutes. The Report of the National Commission on Teachers (1983-85) mooted the idea of Teachers' Centres that could serve as meeting places, where talent could be pooled and teaching experiences shared. It suggested that teachers could go to centres of learning on study leave. The National Policy on Education (1986) linked in-service and pre-service teacher education on a continuum; it visualized the establishment of DIETs in each district, upgradation of 250 colleges of education as Colleges of Teacher Education, and establishment of 50 Institutes of Advanced Studies in Education (IASEs), and strengthening of SCERTs. The Acharya Ramamurthi Review Committee (1990) noted that in-service and refresher courses should be related to specific needs of teachers, and that evaluation and follow up should be part of the scheme.

5.2.5 Initiatives and Strategies forIn-Service Education

Following the NPE (1986), efforts have been made to develop institutions like DIETs, IASEs and CTEs, to provide in-service education to primary and secondary school teachers; 500 DIETs, 87 CTEs and 38 IASEs and 30 SCERTs have been set up, although many of them are yet to function as resource centers. The DPEP also brought in the block and cluster resource centres and made inservice teacher education and cluster level school follow up the main strategies for pedagogic renewal. In spite of the wide spread efforts and specific geographical areas which have shown improvements, by and large the inservice inputs have not had any noticeable impact on teacher practice.

A major indicator of quality of training is its relevance to teachers' needs. But most such programmes are not organized according to actual needs. The approach adopted has remained lecture-based, with little opportunity for trainees to actively participate. Ironically, concepts such as activity-based teaching, classroom management of large classes, multi-grade teaching, team-teaching, and cooperative and collaborative learning, which require active demonstration, are often taught through lectures. School follow-up has also failed to take off, and cluster level meetings have not been able to develop into professional fora for teachers to reflect and plan together.

Any curriculum renewal effort needs to be supported with a well thought out and systematic programme of in-service education and school based teacher support. In-service education cannot be an event but a process, which includes knowledge, development and changes in attitudes, skills, disposition and practice—through interactions both in workshop settings and in the school. It does not consist only of receiving knowledge from experts; promotion of experiential learning, and incorporating teachers as active learners and peer group based review of practice can become a part of the overall strategy. Self-reflection needs to be acknowledged as a vital component of such programmes. A training policy needs to be worked out, defining parameters such as periodicity, context and methodology of programmes. But efforts to strengthen quality and ensure vibrant rather than routinised interactions would require far more decentralized planning with clarity on goals and methods for training and transfer. 'Mass trainings' using new technologies may be of use in some aspects of training, but much greater honesty and bold creativity are required to be able to address the concerns of practising teachers directly including the deprofessionalised environments in which they work, their lack of agency, and alienation.

Dissemination technologies can serve to build a positive ethos for curricular reforms if they are used as sites of discussion and debates in which teachers, training personnel and community members can participate. Teachers require first-hand experience of making programmes themselves in order to develop interest in the new technology. The availability of computers and linkage facilities remains quite inadequate in training institutes. This is one reason why the potential of the new communication technology for changing the ethos of schools and training institutions has remained inadequately tapped.

Pre-service teacher education as well as in-service trainings must build the necessary orientation and capacities in teachers to appreciate, understand and meet the challenges of the curriculum framework. In-service training in particular, must be situated within the context of classroom experiences of teachers. The DIETs, which have the responsibility of organizing such trainings, should do so in a manner in which teachers and their schools benefit from such training. For instance, instead of the adhoc manner in which teacher trainees are sent for in-service training by the educational administration, it would be better for a cluster of schools to be identified and a minimum number of trainees (at least two to enable some peer sharing and reflection) invited from each school to participate in an in-service training. The DIETs, in co-ordination with BRCs could identify the schools for this purpose. In order that teaching time is not unduly affected, and teacher trainees are able to make the link between theory and practice, the mandatory days for training could be split up over the course of the year to include on site work in their own classrooms as well.

Training could comprise a variety of activities in addition to contact lectures and discussions in the teacher training institutions and include workshops in schools in the cluster, projects and other assignments for teachers in their classrooms. To link pre-service and in-service training, the same schools can become sites for preservice internship and student teachers can be asked to observe classroom transaction in these schools. This could serve not only as feedback to teacher educators to strengthen the training programme but can also become the basis of critical reflection by teacher trainees during the latter part of the training programme. To take the process forward, there could be interactive sessions with headmasters from the concerned schools so that they can play the role of a facilitator in the changes in classroom practices that the teacher trainees may like to make. Systems for monitoring and feedback must include SCERT/DIETs/BRCs and CRCs so that academic support can be envisaged in 'follow ups', documentation and research.

5.3 EXAMINATION REFORMS

The report 'Learning without Burden' notes that public examination at the end of Class X and XII should be reviewed with a view to replace prevailing text based and quiz type questioning which induces an inordinate level of anxiety and stress. While urban middle class children are stressed from the need to perform extremely well, rural children are not sure about whether their preparation is adequate even to succeed. The high failure rates, especially among the rural, economically weaker and socially deprived children, forces one to critically review the whole system of evaluation and examination. For if the system were working, there is no reason why children would not progress and learn.

5.3.1 Paper Setting, Examining and Reporting

In order to improve the validity of current examinations, papersetting needs to be rehauled. The focus could shift to *question*setting rather than *paper*-setting. Such questions need not be generated by experts only. Through wide canvassing, good questions can be pooled all year round, from teachers, college professors in that discipline, educators from other states, and even students. These questions, after careful vetting by experts could be categorized, according to level of difficulty, topic area, concept/ competency being evaluated, time estimated to solve. These could be maintained along with a record of usage and testing record, to be drawn on at the time of generating question papers.

Compelling teachers to examine without ensuring adequate compensation makes it difficult to motivate them to ensure better quality and consistency in examining papers. Considering that most boards are in good financial health, funding issues should not come in the way of improving quality. With computerization it is much easier to protect the identity of both examinee and examiner. It is also easier to randomize examination scripts given to any particular examiner, thus checking malpractices. Malpractices such as cheating with help from outside the examination hall can be reduced if candidates are not permitted to leave the exam-centre in the first ninety minutes, and also not permitted to carry question papers out with them while the examination is going on. (The paper can be made available after the examination is over).

Computerisation makes it possible to present a wider range of performance parameters on the marksheet–absolute marks/grades, percentile rank among all candidates of that subject, and percentile rank among peers (*e.g.* schools in the same rural or urban block.). It would also be possible to analyse the quality and consistency of various examiners. The last parameter, in particular, we believe to be a crucial test of merit. Making this information public will allow institutions of higher learning to take a more complex and relativist view of the notion of merit. Such analysis will promote transparency. Requests for re-checks have declined dramatically in places where students have access to their answer papers in either scanned or xeroxed form, on request, for a fee.

In the medium term we need to be able to increasingly shift towards school based assessment, devise ways in which to make such internal assessment more credible. Sensitive teachers usually pick up the unique strengths and weaknesses of students; there should be ways of utilizing such insights. At the same time, to prevent abuse by schools (as is currently the case in practical examinations), they could be graded on a relative, not an absolute, scale and must be moderated and scaled against the marks obtained in the external examination. More research on development, teacher training, and understanding relevant institutional arrangements is required.

5.3.2 Entrances and Board Examinations at Other Levels

Under no circumstances should board or other kinds of whole-block, district or state level examinations be conducted at other grades of schooling, such as class five, eight or eleven. Indeed, even the class X examination can be made optional only for those who wish to continue to class XI, and others may receive a certificate from the school.

There is a need to delink school leaving board examinations from competitive entrance examinations. These examinations can be made less stressful if students had to take fewer of them. A **single nodal agency** could coordinate the design and conduct of these examinations, conducted several times a year, at centres located all over the country, and monitor and ensure the timely conduct and release of student achievement. The scores obtained by students through such a national testing service could be utilized by all institutions for the purpose of admitting students.

5.4 INNOVATION IN IDEAS AND PRACTICES

5.4.1 Plurality of Textbooks

Given the perspective that curricular content must meaningfully incorporate experiences of children and their diverse cultural contexts, including languages, it is important that textbook writing is decentralized keeping in view the capacities that are required as well the systems that will make this possible. The writing of textbooks requires a range of capacities that include academic and research inputs, understanding of children's developmental levels, effective skills of communication and design etc. While the SCERT which presently has been given the task of textbook writing can continue to be the nodal organization for this purpose, the actual envisioning of the process, selection and writing of content must be done in a collaborative manner by teams rather than by individual subject experts. Among the reasons for such a collaborative exercise are perspective building, clarification of assumptions of how children learn, undertaking of the required revisiting of subject knowledge and research input, understanding of processes of how to communicate with children, providing structured space for reflection and feed back by peers as an ongoing process in the making of textbooks and so on. Academic and research support from universities, and the rich experience of nongovernment organsiations as well as practitioners must be important inputs in this exercise.

The 'trailing' of the textbook is extremely critical given that presently children often find text lessons difficult to comprehend, with content that is dense or at times trivial. Lessons are often written without relating them to time that is assigned for the subject to be taught in the school year. It may be a good idea for the initial lessons to be piloted, *i.e.* to be taught on a trial basis with the textbook writer observing its transaction in the class with feedback from both teacher and students. This is also important when innovating with textbook content (for instance providing space to integrate children's experiences) in order to understand and place it within the realities of the classroom and teacher preparation.

It follows that we are ideally looking at the availability of multiple textbooks to schools as they widen teachers' choices and also provide for the incorporation of diversity in relation to children's needs and interests. When a number of books and supplementary materials are available, the teacher can be encouraged to decide which text lessons are appropriate for specific themes for her pupils. This would substantively enhance the teachers' autonomy and choice. Altcrnatively, they can also provide opportunities to encourage children to explore diverse sources and understand how the same content may be presented in different ways. This will encourage library work. The support system that must be ensured will include training programmes/workshops to orient and enable teachers to use textbooks and supplementary materials as resources for curriculum transaction and access to library facilities within the school or in a resource centre for a set of schools. The sharing of libraries between schools must also be consciously planned for and this can be built into partnerships between private and government schools. The setting up of community libraries can also be explored.

Encouraging the production of multiple textbooks, which are officially prescribed by schools, will increasingly bring the private sector into textbook production. In this context it is important to equip state institutions for research and training in education (whose responsibilities include textbooks production) to compete with private publishers and capacities built for this purpose. As mentioned earlier, if SCERTS can make the production of textbooks a collaborative exercise, it will improve the quality of their textbooks, build capacities, as well as energise these institutions. NGOs have also produced excellent textbooks and supplementary materials that can be used in schools. Some thought must also be gives to the regulatory mechanism that must be set in place in order that textbook writers abide by the guiding principles and values of the Constitution (especially equality, secularism and democracy), the aims of education, authenticity and developmental appropriateness of content and so on. In addition it is essential to see that textbook production does not lend itself to private profiteering and deny easy access to education. Discussion of textbooks by parents, teachers and citizens' groups must be encouraged and they must be made available in the public domain (the internet can provide space for this purpose and textbooks can made available on the web) for discussion, feed back, critique etc. Universities can be encouraged to conduct studies of textbooks so that a regular research output on school knowledge is available.

5.4.2 Encouraging Innovations

Individual teachers often explore new ways of transacting the curriculum to address the needs of students within their specific classroom context (including constraints that they may be facing of space, large numbers, absence of teaching aids, diversity in students, the compulsions of examinations and so on). These efforts, often pragmatic but also creative and ingenious, by and large remain invisible to the school and larger teaching community and are usually not valued by teachers themselves. The sharing of teaching experiences and diverse classroom practices can provide opportunities for an academic discourse to develop within schools as teachers interact with and learn from each other. It will also encourage new ideas and facilitate innovation and experimentation. How can innovative and creative ways of teaching and learning be encouraged and supported by the system so that they can become a body of practice that can be brought to a stage when they can be built back into the system? For a start there is a need to create structured spaces within schools, and at the level of the cluster and block where teachers are encouraged to share and discuss classroom practices and experiences. If seen as worthwhile some of these ideas and practices can be systematically followed up. It is also important to bring together groups of teachers within and across schools and provide support to them in terms of resources as well as time to work together. There is also need for documentation and research of identified 'good practices'. Presently there are funds for this purpose both with the DIETs (part of whose mandate is identification and documentation of innovative practices). SSA also has funds for school-based research. Some of this could be used to document diverse practices that teachers use within different classroom contexts. In addition to providing the necessary funding, the creation of an enabling environment that nurtures and provides support to such initiatives is also important. As mentioned carlier efforts to 'mainstream' innovative processes and practices will be necessary.

One of the main objectives of creating resource centers at the cluster level was to break the isolation of individual schools and bring teachers together on a regular basis for sharing their experiences and ideas with their peers. This is important if teachers are to develop their own professional identities and sense of belonging to a larger teaching community. It could also be one way to create among them a sense of their own agency and greater involvement and commitment to their work.

5.4.3 The Use of Technology

The judicious use of technology can increase the reach of educational programmes, facilitate management of the system as well as help address specific learning needs and requirements. For instance, the mass media can be used to support teacher training, facilitate classroom learning and be used for advocacy. Possibilities of teaching and learning at varied paces, self-learning, enabling dual modes of study etc. could all benefit from the use of technology, particularly ICT to enable these processes. The increasing use of internet has enabled sharing of information and providing space for debate and dialogue on diverse issues hitherto unavailable on such a scale. Technological innovations are also necessary for appropriate equipment and aids to meet the learning requirements of children with special needs. What needs to be underscored is that technology could be integrated with the larger goals and processes of educational programmes rather than viewed in isolation or as an add on. In this context technological use which turn teachers and children into mere consumers and technology operators needs to be reviewed and discouraged. Interaction and intimacy is the key to quality education and this cannot be compromised as a principle in any curricular intervention.

5.5 NEW PARTNERSHIPS

5.5.1 Role of NGO, Civil Society Groups, and Teacher organizations

One of the distinct features of the last decade is the increasing involvement of **Non-Government Organisations** and civil society groups in education. NGOs have played a major role in creating innovative models of schooling, training of teachers, development of textbooks and curricular materials, community mobilization and advocacy. Their formal association with schools and resource centres would be extremely important for curriculum development, academic support as well as monitoring and research. Civil society groups have also helped to give education a visible public space and facilitated the emergence of a discourse on the child's right to education. The dissemination of the perspective and ideas of the NCF, their translation into creative and innovative practices within the school and community, critical feedback on different aspects of the curriculum, as well as nurturing of an environment of commitment to the right to education of children, would need collaboration and sustained involvement of diverse civil society groups.

Teachers' associations and organizations can play a far greater role in strengthening school education than has hitherto been the case. For instance they can help evolve norms to improve school functioning by using their influence over their teacher members to ensure that teaching time is not compromised and help create a culture of accountability. They can also draw attention to the inputs and supports that are necessary for effective curriculum transaction and act as constructive pressure groups on issues such as school resources, quality of teacher education and professional development. These associations can work with local level organizations as well as with BRCs and CRCs in defining the nature of academic support required, provide feedback and so on.

Universities have a critical role to play in responding to the broad ranging aims of the curricular framework, especially in the emphasis on encouraging pluralism in education, addressing the needs of children and integrating new curricular areas. There is an urgent need to expand the knowledge base of education keeping in view the diverse socio-cultural contexts to which children belong as well as the complex nature of classroom realities in India. University departments of education, social science as well as the sciences should be urged to include the study of education within their research agenda. Mutli-disciplinary, collaborative research bringing together scholars from different disciplines would be particularly important in generating a research base that is critical for the ideas in the curriculum framework to be translated into enabling classroom practices. At the same time universities need to keep their doors open to children leaving schools with unusual and interesting combinations of study. Rather than using admission criteria to eliminate, they should be open to remain inclusive and encouraging of diversity of interests, pursuits and opportunities. Such open and inclusive admission policies are also crucial if children are to seriously consider vocational courses of study as non-terminal options.

Institutions of higher education have an important role to play in teacher education and enhancing the professional status, not only of secondary school teachers but the elementary stage as well. For the 'reflective teacher' with the professional competence and orientation that the curriculum framework rests on, it will be necessary to review and restructure teacher education programmes. Equally important will be the sustained involvement of scholars in curriculum development, writing and review of textbooks as part of a collaborative exercise, which brings together practitioners and academics with diverse expertise. Higher education can also provide space for reflection, discussion and debate on educational ideas and practices as well as facilitate the interface between schools and policy makers.

There is also need for institutional linkages between universities and institutions such as the SCERT and DIETs to strengthen their **academic programmes of teacher education and in-service training** as well to develop their **research capacities** within. In this context, it would be appropriate to explore again the idea of creating school/ educational complexes that would bring together universities, colleges, schools, SCERT/DIETs as well as non-government organizations within a geographical area to evolve networks and mechanisms **to provide academic support, participate in monitoring, and evaluation of programmes**.

The **preparation of curricula, syllabi and teaching learning resources**, including textbooks, could be carried out in a far greater decentralized and participative manner, increasing the participation of teachers, along with representatives and experts from other organizations. This is especially important when we are exploring to produce more than one textbook for each grade and subject, so that there is far greater local relevance in materials, and also plurality of materials from which teachers can choose. Such large teams could also produce supplementary materials such as reading cards and small stories with local lore and illustrations, which are often more interesting to children. Choice and variety, which exists in more elite schools, can become a common feature of all schools.

The Department of Woman and Child Welfare, Department of Health, Department of Sports and Physical Education, Department of Science and Technology, Tribal and Social Welfare Department, Department of Culture, Tourism, Archeological Survey of India, Panchayati Raj institutions, to name a few, are stakeholders with an interest in children, school, and curriculum. All these departments have the ability to contribute to enriching education for children and teachers. And they need to explore and discover ways in which they can contribute to children's education, converging their inputs with the efforts of departments of education. Not only providing additional facilities to the schools, but funding special programmes that enrich the curriculum, such as **sports clubs** and sports equipment along with special instructors, **visits and excursions** to historical, archeological and natural sites and materials about these places, providing **reference materials**, photographs and charts, (including films and photographs), **ensuring regular health checkups, and monitoring quality of the mid-day meal**, are some of the ways in which these departments can directly contribute to and enhance the quality of the curriculum for children. Educationally meaningful contributions need to be planned in discussion with education departments, rather than independently conceived and simply delivered. This is necessary to ensure that what is being designed is useful and usable. Similarly they could respond to requests made by the department of education for specific programmes or inputs.

OBSERVATIONS

Frequent references are made to the recommendations of Committees and Commissions and especially '*Learning without Burden*'. It appears the document considers this report as the 'Bible' or 'Bhagvad Gita' of education which is to be religiously quoted only!

EPILOGUE

This framework for curriculum presents a vision of what is desirable for our children. It seeks to enable those who are involved with children and their schooling with the bases on which they can make choices that determine the curriculum. This provides an understanding of issues relating to children's learning, the nature of knowledge and the school as an institution. This approach to the curriculum draws attention to the importance of school ethos and culture, the classroom practices of teachers, learning sites outside the school, and learning resources, as much as to the dimensions of the system that exert direct and indirect influence. The designing of large scale curricular interventions, and key activities such as the preparation of syllabus and textbooks and examination reform must be consistent with each other and educational aims for progress and improvement in the quality of education we provide to our children.

Hundreds of parents and teachers sent messages to NCERT in response to advertisements inviting public contributions for the National Curriculum Framework. One of these messages was from a Mumbai-based mother and teacher, Mrs. Neeta Mohla. She wrote:

"Today as students my children face the same learning experiences as me 20 years ago. Everywhere around the world new methods of teaching and evaluation are being practised but our children continue to just copy exercises from the board, mug them up and reproduce them in the exam. If there are changes they are for the worse. Children now have access to more information channels, yet more and more subjects and contents are added to the school bag. Computers, Moral Science etc., etc. recently became hit and G.K. was introduced as a new subject because the quiz show "Kaun Banega Krorepati"...

Our syllabus gets more massive and moves beyond the teaching capacity of the teachers so they rush through the contents with tedious methodology. Students cannot meet the attention span requirement in the classrooms and either fail at comprehension or blank out into daydreaming. Newer topics of many different subjects are covered even before the previous ones have been chewed over. The burden of the syllabus is then passed on to the parents or tuition classes. Little children burdened with loads of 'education' on their shoulders trip from school to tuition classes, bypassing childhood. A section of students study harder and harder to beat each other for the top slot. Majority of the students are hounded by parents and teachers to study harder and become stressed, some requiring even clinical treatment. Only children who excel in the main subjects are regarded as successful. Children with accomplishments in other fields like sports and arts are underrated. They are earnestly discouraged from pursuing sports and hobbies as these don't count in the mark list. The curriculum and success dynamics demand that they shut out the real world with real experiences and lock themselves up in the world of books. Even 6th std. students must study 4 hours in addition to school hours if they want to enter into the race for marks.

When children in their developmental years spend more time in books than in the real world, they have every chance of becoming fragmented. Education ventures into a negative course. It splits a student's mind into two. A bookish worldview that he memorizes without proper comprehension and the real world that is not in his/her control due to lack of focus. Take the example of a typical fourth standard child; he knows how stopping cattle grazing on hilltops can prevent soil erosion but he cannot keep track of his/her notebooks and pencils. Ultimately he grows into an adult with a lot of knowledge sense but no common sense, a "padha likha bevakoof" (an educated fool). Good characters and personalities develop through focus on their development. Instead, a lot is taught which he cannot relate with his/her day-to-day life experiences and surroundings. For those who blank out into daydreaming education fails to make any impression, leaving them vulnerable to other dangerous influences. There is no support system for children in need of it. Parents today are just as stressed as their wards. A staggering 75 per cent children preparing for Board Examinations today suffer from stress related disorders." Her write-up gives several concrete suggestions, some of which are the following:

- Balance what should be taught in favour of what can possibly be learnt. The structures of nature are architectural marvels wherein each part functions in coordination with the whole. The real challenge is to plan the curriculum so that it has the main elements that work to keep broad objectives of education in course and are well grounded in the realities of availabilities and constraints.
- Instead of a structure built to promote success for a select few, we must adopt a structure that engages participation in learning by all. The base should be sturdy so it lasts a whole life. The pillars should be broadened and redefined. New pillars like personality, character, physical fitness, creative and critical thinking should be laid alongside the old academic pillars of maths, science, history etc.
- Contents must be linked to the challenges of life and career at different stages. Students and teachers must be given the

requisite time to focus on them. Acquisition of pure knowledge should be for the purpose of self discovery of the child's own interest. This should be covered through alternative study methodology like project method and alternative evaluation models like open book exams. We need only implant the seeds of every subject. Whole plants do not have to be hammered in. Education should inspire children to become learners for life.

- We must humanise education and make it relevant for the pursuit of the wide variety of human aptitudes. Alternative evaluation and grading models must be sought to encourage the diversity of talents among the learners. Achievers in sports, arts and crafts should get due recognition at par with academic achievers. Expanding the achievement list would definitely de-stress parents and children by spreading them out on to more tracks. The change in grading would immediately shift the society's focus on the Darwinian implications of curriculum framework.

Let us hope curriculum, syllabi and textbook designers across the country will pay adequate and urgent attention to this mother's words.

OBSERVATIONS

It is common knowledge that State Boards suggest/prescribe a number of textbooks which provide ample scope for selection for teachers.

There is nothing new in the message sent to NCERT by a Mumbai based mother.

In the last analysis it must be accepted that education is a subject on which everybody has to say something. It is usually not appreciated that education is a subsystem of social system and its functioning should be seen in the overall functioning of economico-politico-socio system of the country. The functioning of the present system of education is in no way inferior to the functioning of other subsystems. Of course this does not mean that there is no room for improvement in education. Constant criticism of the system serves little perpose.

OBSERVATIONS

The title of the Document 'National Curriculum Framework 2005' appears to be deceptive for it does not indicate whether it pertains to school education or higher education. The earlier document was aptly titled 'National Curriculum Framework for School Education'.

7

Overall Observations on the Document and the Need for the Try-out of the Proposed Curriculum

The NCF is the outcome of much hard labour of some of the topmost educational theorists, planners and administrators of the country. It covers a vast gamut of crucial parameters of the curriculum. It makes a brief survey of the educational scenario and the efforts made in the past in the restructuring of the curriculum. It contains several excellent recommendations on the various dimensions of the curriculum and related issues. It should serve as a standard textbook of for pre-service and in-service education of teachers.

In the first instance it is pertinent to refer to observations made by Udayan Namboodiri, a Senior Editor of 'the *Pioneer*': "...the NCERT's own academic staff, passed a resolution on the previous evening (June 6, 2005) condemning the "draft" which was going in the NCERT's name. This was unprecedented." (*Organiser*, June 13-19, 2005). The NCERT, However, did not respond to the communication which was made to it with respect to these observations.

As regards its successful implementation, it does not generate strong optimism for it fails to suggest any time-bound programme based on the availability of funds. Specific resource-based deadlines are missing. It is very unfortunate that it does not provide any clue as to how requisite funding of the mammoth order for its implementations is to be achieved.

The document is full of fashionable verbiage and high platitudes. 'Parrot-like' repetition is made of the recommendations of the '*Learning without Burden*' (1993).

The CBSE curriculum presently in use covers almost all the features of the proposed NCF. The CBSE takes due care of updating it, revising it, and incorporating changes in the evaluation practices. Of course there is always scope for improvement.

We have had many such outstanding documents in the past. But what we need to-day is a more concrete and effective 'Programme of Action' for implementation.

One is reminded of the words of wisdom of Dr. Manmohan Singh. In an article entitled '*Education: a Development View*', he succinctly observed, "So much has been said, suggested and recommended that when it comes to implementation, the budgetary constraints make a mincemeat of our educational aspirations... We have to be perhaps ruthlessly realistic about our economic and budgetary constraints. There is no point in trying to apply one cubic inch of butter to a square mile of bread. Such an attempt would imply a realignment of priorities in educational investment and discarding a part of the band wagon." (*Hindustan Times*', March 22, 1986).

TRY-OUT OF NCF

Having said all this, it is felt that the NCF should be given a fair trial. A broad outline of the try-out may be on the following pattern.

Almost every State has a State Institute of Education/SCERT. Its staff is supposed to be quite experienced. One government school in each state should be put under the charge of each SCERT. In operational terms, for all purposes, the school should be run by the SCERT for one year during period of try-out. Regular school staff should be substituted by SCERT staff.

Likewise each of the five NCERTs Regional Institutes should adopt a school.

The Headquarter staff of the NCERT staff, may also adopt five to ten government schools in Delhi for trying out the curriculum.

Likewise, NCTE should also be assigned this work.

The staff should be deputed to work in their own pay-scales and given all the facilities they enjoy.

Simultaneously the NCF should be tried out in about forty government schools in different States with the regular/normal school staff.

The results of the try-outs should be evaluated after one year and on this basis, NCF may be implemented in all the schools.

Central Institute of Education, Delhi may also try-out the curriculum.

An additional 5 per cent grant may be given for carrying out the try-out of NCF. the modalities of the try-out can be suitably worked out.

8

Major Observations and Recommendations of National Curriculum Framework—NCF (2005)

INTRODUCTION

The NCF was approved by the Central Advisory Board of Education in September 2005. A detailed analysis of the NCF has been made in the preceding Chapters. Here a summary of the major observations and recommendation is provided to have a quick but meaningful review.

I. Aims of Education

The NCF 2005 sets out the following aims of education:

- Commitment to democratic values of equality, justice and freedom.
- Concern for other's well-being.
- Secularism
- Respect for human dignity and rights.

II. Guiding Principles of Curriculum Construction

- Connecting knowledge to life outside the school
- Ensuring that learning is shifted away from rote methods.
- Enriching the curriculum to provide for overall development of children rather than remain textbooks centric.
- Making examination more flexible and integrated with classroom life.

III. Approach to Knowledge in the Curriculum

- Acquiring a critical perspective on social reality and the natural environment, through the lenses provided by the subject matter.

- Connecting with the local, and conceptualized in order to 'situate' knowledge and realizing its relevance and meaningfulness, to reaffirm one's experiences outside school; to draw one's learning from observing, interacting with, classifying; categorizing, to question, reason and argue in relation to these experiences.
- Making connections across disciplines and bringing out the interrelatedness of knowledge.
- Realizing the 'fruitfulness' and 'openness' of enquiry, and the provisional nature of truths.
- Engaging with 'local knowledge'/indigenous and practices in the local area, and relating these to school knowledge wherever possible.
- Encouraging questions and leaving space open for the pursuit of new questions.
- Being sensitive to the issues of 'equality' to classroom transaction as well as established stereotypes and discrimination, regarding learnability of the knowledge area by different groups (e.g. girls not given field based projects, blindly excluded from the option of learning mathematics, etc.)
- Developing the imagination, and keeping imagination and fantasy alive.

IV. Learner Centred Curriculum (Learning and Knowledge)

- Reorienting our perception of learners and learning.
- Holistic approach in the treatment of learners' development and learning/adopting.
- Meeting learning disability needs through data based and need specific programmes.
- Engaging learners in the construction of knowledge and fostering creativity.
- Making learning active through experimental mode.
- Providing adequate room for voicing children's thinking, curiosity and questions in curricular practices.
- Connecting knowledge across discipline boundaries to provide a broader frame for insightful construction of knowledge.
- Adopting various forms of learner engagement-observing, exploring, discovering, analyzing, critical reflection, etc. are as important as the content of knowledge.
- Planning Activities for developing critical perspectives on socio-cultural realities need to find space in curriculum practices.
- Making local knowledge and children's experiences as essential components of textbooks and pedagogic practices.

- Taking into account school years as a period of rapid development with changes and shifts in capabilities, attitudes and interests that have implications for choosing and organizing the content and process of knowledge.

V. Curriculum Areas: School Stages and Assessment

1. *Languages*

- Taking note of the fact that language skills-speech and listening, reading and writing-cut across school subjects and disciplines. Their foundational role in children's construction of knowledge right from elementary classes through senior secondary classes needs to be recognized.
- Making renewed effort to implement the three-language formula, emphasizing recognition of children's mother tongue(s) as the best medium of instruction. These include tribal languages.
- Keeping in view that success in learning English is possible only if it builds on sound language pedagogy in the mother tongue.
- Seeing multilingual character of Indian society as a resource for enrichment of school life.

2. *Mathematics*

- Considering mathematization (ability to think logically, formulate and handle abstraction) rather than 'Knowledge' of mathematics (formals and mechanical procedures) as the main goal of teaching mathematics.
- Enhance the child's ability to think and reason, to visualize and handle abstractions, to formulate and solve problems. Access to quality mathematics education is the right of every child.

3. *Science*

- Making content, process and language of science teaching commensurate with learner's agc-range and cognitive reach.
- Engaging the learner in acquiring methods and process that will nurture their curiosity and creativity, particularly in relation to the environment.
- Placing science teaching in the wider context of children's environment to equip them with requisite knowledge and skills to enter the world of work.
- Permeating of environmental concerns through the entire school curriculum.

4. *Social Science*

- Equipping children with moral and mental energy so as to provide them the ability to think independently and reflect critically on social issues.
- Promoting interdisciplinary approaches, to key national concerns such as gender justice, human rights and sensitivity to marginalized groups and minorities.
- Recasting civics as political science, and recognizing the history as a shaping influence on the child's conception of the past and civic identity.

5. *Work*

- Infusing work in all subjects from the primary stage upwards.
- Formally recognizing agencies and settings offering work opportunities outside the school.
- Designing Vocational Education and Training (VET) programme based on the perspective of 10-12 years of work centre education with in-built features of:
  - Flexible and modular course of varying durations
  - Multiple entry and exits points
  - Accessibility from the level of village clusters to district levels.
  - Decentralized accreditation and equivalence mechanism for agencies located outside the school system.

6. *Art*

- Recognising arts (folk and classical forms of music and dance, visual arts, puppetry, clay, work, theatre, etc.) and heritage crafts as integral components of the school curriculum.
- Building awareness of their relevance to personal, social, economic and aesthetic needs among parents, school authorities and administrators.
- Compring the arts as a subject at every stage of school education.

7. *Peace*

- Promoting peace-oriented values in all subjects throughout school years with the help of relevant activities.
- Forming peace education a component of teacher education.

8. *Health and Physical Education*

- Health and Physical education are necessary for the overall development of learners. Through health and physical education programmes (including yoga), it may be possible to handle successfully the issues of enrolment, retention and completion of school.

VI. School and Classroom Environment

- Accepting that availability of minimum infrastructure and material facilities, and support for planning a flexible daily schedule are critical for improved teacher performance.
- Providing a school culture that nurtures children's identities as 'learners' and enhances the potential and interests of each child.
- Undertaking specific activities and ensuring participation of all children—able and disabled.
- Developing the value of self-discipline among learners through democratic functioning.
- Assuring the participation of community members in sharing knowledge and experience in a subject area as it helps in forging a partnership between school and community.
- Reconceptualizing learning resources in terms of:
  - Textbooks focused on elaboration of concepts, activities, problems and exercises encouraging reflective thinking and group work.
  - Supplementary books, workbooks, teachers' handbooks, etc. based on fresh thinking and new perspectives.
  - Multimedia and ICT as sources for two-way interaction rather than one-way reception.
  - School library as an intellectual space for teachers, learners and members of the community to deepen their knowledge and connect with the wider world.
- Decentralizing planning of school calendar and daily schedule and autonomy for teacher professionalism practices as these are basic to creating a learning environment.

VII. Systematic Reforms

- Considering quality, a key feature of systemic reform and which implies the system's capacity to reform itself by enhancing its ability to remedy its own weaknesses and to develop new capabilities.
- Preparing a broad framework for planning upwards, beginning with schools for identifying focus areas and subsequent consolidation at the cluster and block levels could form a

decentralized planning strategy at the district level.

- Making academic planning in a participatory manner by headmasters and teachers.
- Monitoring quality to be seen as a process of sustaining interaction with individual schools in terms of teaching-learning process.
- Strengthening professional training of teachers by linking it to:
  - post-graduate studies in different subjects.
  - provisions for integrated undergraduate studies in teacher education.
  - inclusion of a course on language proficiency as an integral component.
  - engaging the trainees with the larger context of education, interacting with children in real contexts and critically questioning their own beliefs about knowledge and learning, gender, caste, equity and justice, shifting the focus from pure disciplinary knowledge to the learner and his/her context.
- Making in-service education a catalyst for change in school practices.
- Strengthening Panchayati Raj system by evolving a mechanism to regulate the functioning of parallel bodies at the village level so that democratic participation in development can be realized.

VIII. Examination Reforms

- Reducing stress and enhancing success in examination necessitate:
  - Shift from content-based testing to problem-solving and understanding. For this to happen the present typology of the question paper must change.
  - Shift toward shorter examinations.
  - Setting up of a single nodal agency for coordinating the design and conduct of entrance examinations.
- Making multiple textbooks available to widen teachers's choices and provide for the diversity in childrens' needs and interests.
- Sharing of teaching experiences and diverse classroom practices to generate new ideas and facilitate innovation and experimentation.
- Developing syllabi, textbooks and teaching learning resources in a decentralized and participatory manner involving teachers, experts from universities, NGOs and teachers' organizations.

9

Curriculum Construction and Central Board of Secondary Education (CBSE), Delhi

Introduction

There are more than 40 Boards of School Education in India and each of these boards is an autonomous body which prepares its own curriculum. Of-course, the NCF prepared by the NCERT remains the basis.

The Central Board of Secondary Education, Delhi is usually considered as the pace setting Board in the country. It has its own mechanism in this regard. The CBSE is a very dynamic and progressive Board. It does not wait for the NCERT curriculum which is normally updated after a pretty long period. The CBSE updates its curriculum regularly.

The curriculum prepared by NCERT has no legal sanction behind it but the CBSE curriculum must be followed by the schools affiliated to it.

The CBSE also circulates a list of recommended/suggestived books at the secondary and senior secondary stages of education.

About 6 per cent of secondary/higher secondary schools in the country are affiliated to CBSE.

All boards in the country are expected to update their curriculum and incorporate contents in the light of new demands on education.

Historical Background

A trail of developments mark the significant changes that took place over the years in shaping up the Board to its present status. U.P. Board of High School and Intermediate Education was the first Board set up in 1921. It had under its jurisdiction Rajputana, Central India and Gwalior also. In response to the representation made by the Government of United Provinces, the then Government of India suggested to set up a joint Board in 1929 for all the areas and this was named as the "Board of High School and Intermediate Education, "Rajputana". This included Ajmer, Merwar, Central India and Gwalior.

The Board witnessed rapid growth and expansion at the level of secondary education resulting in improved quality and standard of education in its institutions. But with the advent of State Universities and State Boards in various parts of the country the jurisdiction of the Board was confined only to Ajmer, Bhopal and Vindhya Pradesh. As a result of this, in 1952, the constitution of Board was amended wherein its jurisdiction was extended to part-C and part-D territories and the Board was given its present name "Central Board of Secondary Education". It was in the year 1962 finally that the Board was reconstituted. At present about 6,200 schools are affiliated to the Board.

Jurisdiction

The jurisdiction of the Board is extensive and stretches beyond the national geographical boundaries. As a result of the reconstruction, the erstwhile "Delhi Board of Secondary Education" was merged with the Central Board and thus all the educational institutions recognised by the Delhi Board also became a part of the Central Board. Subsequently, all the schools located in the Union Territory of Chandigarh, Andaman and Nicobar Islands, Arunachal Pradesh and the state of Sikkim got affiliation with the Board.

Major Objectives

- To prescribe conditions of examinations and conduct public examinations at the end of Class X and XII. To grant qualifying certificates to successful candidates of the affiliated schools.
- To fulfill the educational requirements of those students whose parents are employed in transferable jobs.
- To prescribe and update the courses of instruction for examinations.
- To affiliate institutions for the purpose of examination and raise the academic standards of the country.

The Board Also Promotes

Innovations in teaching learning methodologies by devising student friendly and student centered paradigms:

- Reforms in examinations and evaluation practices.
- Skill learning by adding job oriented and job linked inputs.
- Regularly updating the pedagogical skills of the teachers and

administrators by conducting inservice training programmcs, workshops, etc.

Scheme of Studies at the Secondary Stage (Class IX and X, 2007-9)

Subjects of Studies

The learning areas will include :

1 and 2. Two Languages out of : Hindi, English, Assamese, Bengali, Gujrati, Kannada, Kashmiri, Marathi, Malayalam Manipuri, Oriya, Punjabi, Sindhi, Tamil, Telugu, Urdu, Lepcha, Limbu, Bhutia, Sanskrit Arabic, Persian, French, German, Portuguese, Russian, Spanish, Nepali, Tibetan and Mizo, (Please also refer to notes) (i), (ii) and (iii)

3. Mathematics
4. Science and Technology
5. Social Science
6. Work Education or Pre-Vocational Education
7. Art Education
8. Physical and Health Education

Additional Subjects

Students may offer any one of the following as an additional subject :

Language other than the two compulsory languages (offered as subjects of study)

Or

Commerce, Painting, Music, Home Science or Introductory Information Technology.

Notes

(i) It is expected that all the students would have studied three languages upto class VIII. Those students who could not clear the third language in class VIII, and have been promoted to class IX shall be examined by the schools concerned at the end of class IX in the same syllabus and text books as are prescribed for class VIII. Those who are still unable to clear the third language at the end of class IX may be given another opportunity in class X. No student shall be eligible to appear at the Secondary School Examination of the Board at the end of class X unless he/she has cleared the third language.

(ii) Hindi and English must be two of the three languages to be offered as stated in the note. (i) above. Hindi and English must have been studied at least upto class VIII.

(iii) Hindi and English must be one of the two languages to be studied in class IX and X Hindi and English can also be offered simultaneously. In Hindi and English, two courses have been provided for class IX and X keeping in view the varying background of the student. A student may either opt Communicative- English (Subject Code 101) or English Language and Literature (Subject Code 184). Similarly, in Hindi, a student may either opt for Hindi A or Hindi B.

Instructional Time

Assuming an academic week consisting of 45 periods of 40 minutes duration each, the broad distribution of periods per week will be as follows:

Subjects	*Suggested Periods for Class X*
Language I	7
Language II	6
Mathematics	7
Science and Technology	9
Social Science	9
Work Education or Pre-Vocational Education	6 (3+3)*
Art Education	2
Physical and Health Education	2

* Time Expected to be spent outside school hours.

Note: While designing the courses it has been presumed that, given margin for vacations, public holidays and other contingencies, a minimum of 30 weeks of teaching time will be available in each session for actual instructional transaction. Accordingly the distribution of periods over units and sub-units has been done which is only suggestive in character. The school, keeping the overall number of periods in each subject/area the same, may assign more or less number of periods to individual units according to their relative importance, if thought necessary. The distribution of marks over each unit (unit wise weightage), is however, prescriptive hence shall remain, unchanged.

Special Adult Literacy Drive (SALD)

In pursuance of the objectives of National Literacy Mission, Govt. of India, Special Adult Literacy programme has been taken up by the Board from the academic session 1991-92 beginning with classes IX & XI as special measure to remove illiteracy through mass involvement of students.

This has been termed as SALD. The SALD has been made an integral part of prescribed curriculum and incorporated in work-education as an essential component.

Scheme of Studies (2009) at the Senior Secondary Stages—Classes XI-XII

Academic Stream

The learning areas will include:

I&II Two Languages (Core/Elective) out of

Hindi, English, Assamese, Bengali, Gujrati, Kashmiri, Kannada, Marathi, Malyalam, Manipuri, Oriya, Punjabi, Sindhi, Tamil, Telugu, Urdu, Sanskrit, Arabic, Persian, Limboo, Lepcha, Bhutia, Nepali, Tibetan, French, German, Portuguese, Russian and Spanish.

Notes: 1. Out of the languages, one shall be English or Hindi, both English and Hindi can also be offered simultaneously.

2. The languages may be offered either at Core/Elective level. The same language, however cannot be' offered both at the Core level and Elective level.
3. A candidate has the freedom to offer, in lieu of one of the two languages above, any other elective subject provided under III below.

Note: English can be offered at any of the three levels given below:

1. English Core
2. English Elective
3. Functional English

III to V. Three Elective out of the following:

Mathematics, Physics, Chemistry, Biology, Biotechnology, Engineering Drawing, Economics, Political Science, History, Geography, Business Studies, Accountancy, Home Science, Fine Arts, Agriculture, Computer Science/Informatics Practices, Multimedia and Web Technology, Sociology, Psychology, Philosophy, Physical Education, Music and Dance, Entrepreneurship, Fashion Studies, Environmental Education. (In this regard please also refer to notes below).

Note: 1. The candidate shall opt either for Computer Science or Informatics Practices. However along with either of this, they can opt for Multimedia and Web technology. Thus, a candidate can opt for maximum of two IT based Courses.

VI. General Studies

VII. Work Experience

VIII. Physical and Health Education

Additional Subject

A candidate can also offer an additional elective which may either be a language at elective level (out of those mentioned above) or, any other elective subject.

While transacting the Curriculum due emphasis should be laid on National Identity and Value Education. Schools are expected to draw their own programmes in this area in accordance with the guidelines contained in the brochure 'National Integration through Schools' published by the Board. Likewise, programmes in General Studies, Work Experience and Physical and Health Education be planned in accordance with the guidelines brought out by the Board.

Bridges between Vocational and Academic Streams

Bridges between Commerce-based vocational courses/packages and the subjects pertaining to different disciplines under the Academic Stream have also been provided. Accordingly, Business Studies, Accountancy and other subjects can be combined, subject to meeting the obligations required under the prescribed scheme of studies, with the following arcas from the Commerce based Vocational Courses:

1. Typewriting in English (code no. 607)
2. Stenography in English (code no. 608)
3. Typewriting in Hindi (code no. 609)
4. Stenography in Hindi (code no. 610)
5. Marketing (code no. 613)
6. Consumer Behaviour and Protection (code no. 615)
7. Storekeeping (code no. 617)
8. Store Accounting (code no. 618)

Note:These electives can be offered along with Business Studies, Accountancy and other subject to the following stipulations:

(i) Not more than two electives from the above list be offered.

(ii) These papers be not combined with the electives related to similar disciplines under the academic stream in order to avoid duplication e.g. Store Accounting (code no. 618) cannot be combined with Accountancy (code no. 055)

(iii) If Stenography in Hindi or English is offered, it is obligatory to offer Hindi Typewriting or English Typewriting respectively as the case may be to make the combinations more meaningful. English Stenography, however, cannot be combined with Hindi Typewriting or corollarily Hindi Stenography with English Typewriting.

Instructional Time

Subject	*Suggestive Periods*
Language I	7
Language II	7
Elective I	8
Elective II or Vocational Course	8
Elective III	8
General Studies/General Foundation Course (GFC)	3
Work Experience (Not applicable to Vocational Stream)	2+2*
Physical & Health Education	2

* Time expected to spend outside school hours

While designing the courses it has been presumed that, given margin to vacations, public holidays and other contingencies, a minimum of 30 weeks of teaching time will be available in each session for actual instructional transaction. Accordingly, the distribution of periods over units and sub-units has been made which is only suggestive in character. The schools, keeping the overall number of periods in each subject area the same may assign more or less number of periods to individual units according to their relative importance if throughout necessary. The distribution of marks over each unit (unitwise weightage) is perspective, hence shall remain unchanged.

Notes: 1. Schools are expected to give adequate time for Community Service outside the school hours, the minimum being equivalent of two periods a week.

2. The Vocational Group candidates should make use of the time allotted for Work Experience for on the job training, if so required.

Medium of Instruction

The medium of instruction in general in all the schools affiliated with the board shall either be English or Hindi.

Special Adult Literacy Drive (SALD)

In pursuance of the objects of the National Literacy Mission, Government of India, a Special Adult Literacy Programme has been taken up by Board from the academic session 1991-92 beginning with classes IX & XI as a special measure to help remove illiteracy, through massive involvement of students. This has been termed as SALD. The Adult Literacy Drive has been made an essential component of Work Experience.

Grading

(i) Assessment of theory/practical papers in external subjects shall be in numerical scores. In addition to numerical scores, the Board shall indicate grade in the marks sheets issued to the candidates in case of subjects of external examinations. In case of internal assessment subject only grades shall be shown.

(ii) Letter grades on a nine-point scale shall be used.

(iii) The grades shall be derived from scores in case of subjects of external examination. In case of subjects of internal assessment, they shall be awarded by the schools.

(iv) The qualifying marks in each subject of external examination shall be 33% at Senior School Certificate Examination. However, at Senior School Certificate Examination, in a subject involving practical work, a candidate must obtain 33% marks in the theory and 33% marks in the practical separately in addition to 33% marks in aggregate, in order to qualify in that subject.

(v) For awarding the grades, the Board shall put all the passed students in a rank order and will award grades as follows:

A-I	Top 1/8th of the passed candidates
A-2	Next 1/8th of the passed candidates
B-1	Next 1/8th of the passed candidates
B-2	Next 1/8th of the passed candidates
C-l	Next 1/8th of the passed candidates
C-2	Next 1/8th of the passed candidates
D-l	Next 1/8th of the passed candidates
D-2	Next 1/8th of the passed candidates
E	Failed Candidates

Notes:

(a) Minor variation in proportion of candidates to adjust ties will be made.

(b) In case of a tie, all the students getting the same score, will get the same grade. If the number of students at a score point need to be divided into two segments, the smaller segment will go with the larger.

(c) Method of grading will be used in subjects where the number of candidates who have passed is more than 500.

(d) In respect of subjects where total number of candidates passing in a subject is less than 500, the grading would be adopted on the pattern of grading and distribution in other similar subjects.

Scheme of Examination (Senior School Certificate Examination)

(i) The Board shall conduct examination in all subjects except General Studies, Work Experience, Physical and Health Education, which will be assessed internally by the schools.

(ii) In all subjects examined by the Board, a student will be given one paper each carrying 100 marks for 3 hours. However, in subjects requiring practical examination, there will be a theory paper and practical examinations as required in the syllabi and courses.

(iii) In Work Experience, General Studies and Physical and Health Education, the Schools will maintain cumulative records of student's periodical achievements and progress during the year. These records are subject to the scrutiny of the Board as and when deemed fit.

(iv) A candidate from a recognised school who has some physical deformity or is otherwise unable to take part in Work Experience and Physical and Health Education, may be granted exemption by the Chairman on the recommendation of the Head of the institution, supported by the medical certificate from a Medical Officer of the rank not below an Assistant Surgeon.

(v) Private/Patrachar Vidyalaya and candidates sponsored by Adult School shall be exempted from Work Experience, General Studies and Physical and Health Education.

(vi) A candidate may offer an additional subject which can be either a language at elective level or another elective subject as prescribed in the Scheme of Studies, subject to the conditions laid down in the Pass Criteria.

Pass Criteria (Senior School Certificate Examination)

(i) A candidate will be eligible to get the pass certificate of the Board, if he/she gets a grade higher than E in all subjects of internal assessment unless he/she is exempted. Failing this, result of the external examination will be withheld but not for a period of more than one year.

(ii) In order to be declared as having passed the examination, a candidate shall obtain a grade higher than E (i.e. at least 33% marks) in all the five subjects of external examination in the main or at the end of the compartmental examination. The pass marks in each subject of external examination shall be 33%. In case of a subject involving practical work a candidate must obtain 33% marks in theory and 33% marks in practical separately in addition to 33% marks in aggregate in order to qualify in that subject.

(iii) No overall division/distinction/aggregate shall be awarded.

(iv) In respect of a candidate offering an additional subject, the following norms shall be applied:

- (a) A language offered as an additional subject may replace a language in the event of a candidate failing in the same provided after replacement the candidate has English/ Hindi as one of the languages.
- (b) An elective subject offered as an additional subject may replace one of the elective subjects offered by the candidate. It may also replace a language provided after replacement the candidate has English/Hindi as one of the languages.
- (c) Additional language offered at elective level may replace an elective subject provided after replacement, the number of languages offered shall not exceed two.

(v) Candidates exempted from one or more subjects of internal examination shall be eligible for appearing in external examination and result shall be declared subject to fulfilment of other conditions laid down in the Pass Criteria.

(vi) In order to be declared as having passed the Class XI Examination a candidate shall obtain 33% marks in all the subjects. The pass marks in each subject of examination shall be 33%. In case of subject involving practical work a candidate must obtain 33% marks in theory and 33% in practical separately in addition to 33% marks in aggregate in order to qualify in that subject.

10

Curriculum and Textbooks

Present Status Regarding Educational Policies, Curriculum Framework and Textbooks: Institutional Mechanism

Educational policies are prepared by the committees set up by the Ministry of Human Resources Development, placed before the Central Advisory of Education (CABE) for it approval and tabled in both the Houses of Parliament for their approval. The Committees usually consider the reports of the Education Commission/Commissions. Milestones in policy include the report of the Education Commission (1964-66), published under the title **'Education and National Development'**, National Policy on Education (1968), NPE 1986 and amended in 1992. On the basis of these policies, the NCERT designs the National Curriculum Framework (NCF). The NCERT has so far produced four sets of curriculum and syllabi (1975, 1988, 2002 and 2005). In the light of the curriculum, textbooks are prepared. Here it may be emphasized that the curriculum serves as a guide for the preparation of textbooks. As a matter of fact, curriculum, in itself has no significance, apart from textbooks. Text books are the most important means of operationalising the curriculum. In the earlier chapters, various aspects relating to curriculum are detailed. Here, the mechanism of textbooks production and their use is discussed in brief.

State Governments started to assume charge of the production of textbooks after the Education Commission (1964-66) drew attention to the factors contributing to the neglect of this area—lack of interest by scholars, unscrupulous publishers and unaffordable prices, irregularities in the selection and prescription of books and the lack of supporting materials like teachers' guides.

Most states have created bodies through legislation for the preparation of syllabi and textbooks. They have also established mechanisms for the approval and preparation of textbooks. However the procedure varies in states.

In Punjab and Tamil Nadu, textbooks for all classes are prepared and published by *one State-controlled body*. In Sikkim and Haryana, the State Institution of Education/the NCERT prepares books only for primary classes, adopting the NCERT books for higher classes (or private publishers for middle school). Andhra Pradesh uses textbooks from the centrally funded and controlled DPEP, SSA till Class Eight, and its SCERT's books for Classes Nine and Ten.

In Mizoram, the Board conducting examinations prepares all the books it prescribes. In Orissa, the autonomous Board of Secondary Education prepares books for Classes Eight to Ten, after which the State Bureau of Textbook Preparation and Publication takes over. In both Kamataka and Gujarat, SCERTs are strongly *state-controlled.*

Board monopolizes publication and distribution, while in Karnataka 40 percent; of the textbooks are given to private publishers to print.

In Uttar Pradesh, the Parishads for Basic and Madhyamik Shiksha approve a panel of authors, and schools *are free to choose* books by any one, books being published privately. The Madhya Pradesh Textbook Act (1973, 1974) states that even private schools affiliated to the State Board should follow SCERT publications (the government seeks also to monitor library books), but in practice, only those taking public examinations follow this.

The public examination comprises the sole but significant link between private unaided schools and state government authorities.

Many states, like Delhi, Karnataka, Madhya Pradesh and West Bengal get school teachers, subject experts, members from DIETs and voluntary organizations to collaborate on textbook preparation. Some states have elaborate procedures for approval—West Bengal and Gujarat undertake a phased trial of textbooks in schools before finalizing manuscripts. In Kamataka, manuscripts are submitted to a second group of experts and introduced in certain blocks of the state before final revisions. In Rajasthan, manuscripts are presented to the Education Secretary and Education Minister. In Madhya Pradesh, the government notifies the books for government primary and upper primary schools after their approval by the (government convened) textbook standing committee. While mechanisms for regulation are in place in Bihar, there is insufficient co-ordination between the agencies responsible for preparing textbooks, and the government's failure to produce books on time has left the field clear for private publishers.

Across states, there thrives on the prescribed material a private industry circulating shadows of government books, teachers' handbooks, "question banks" and guides. The last are sometimes twice the price of government books (the majority of children buy both, starting as early as Class Four). Guides comprise the main private publications mentioned in the report from Karnataka, where even private schools adhere mainly to government books. Jammu and Kashmir has no major private publishers within the state and the private publications favored in Kerala's English medium schools are those with a pan-Indian market.

Textbooks and curricula in schools run by religious and social organizations and schools not aided by the state are not regulated in any form by state agencies. Some of them use this route to promote ideologies that often contradict the basic principles and vision of the Constitution and educational policies. One disturbing fact is that the free space permitted in the system is often abused for partisan purposes by sectarian organizations and schools affiliated to them.

Limited Use of NCERT Textbooks

Although the NCERT texts are used all over India, these are, however, limited to schools affiliated to the Central Board of Secondary Education (CBSE) and the number of schools which accept this scheme remains small. Out of a total number of around 1,25,000 recognized secondary and higher secondary schools in the country about 6200 are at present under the CBSE. Even those that use the CBSE syllabi, do so largely for the higher classes for the purpose of Board examinations.

Need for Improvement in Textbooks

There is an urgent need to ensure that the education system reflects the secularnationalistic discourse; it must remain free of communalism; it must reflect the cultural diversity of our nation and the multicultural nature of our society; and it must not exacerbate gender, caste and community inequalities. The very diversity and inequality of Indian society is a compelling reason to address with urgency the questions of social equality, multiple identities and national identity and their presentation in educational materials. One of the most important means of promoting equity in a democratic society is to make good critical education available to all. This requires curricular frameworks that reflect these objectives. These then need to be translated into textbooks.

The commitment towards achieving equality through education—a central concern of the national endeavour underlying Indian education—has been unequivocally voiced in all the major policy documents of independent India. The task of translating this vision of equality into a curricular framework and into textbooks is challenging enough and remains not fully realized. In other words, we have not always been able to concretise the conceptions and policy statements and embody these into a democratic curriculum, which is reflected in textbooks. The concerted sectarianism and communalist politics of the recent past have made this task doubly difficult.

Appointment of the CABE Committee (2004-2005)

The Government of India reconstituted the CABE vide Resolution 6.7.2004. The first meeting was held on August 10-11, 2004. After extensive discussions on several critical issues connected with education in this meeting, the Minister of Human Resources Development set up seven Committees to deal with important issues pertaining to different aspects of school, higher and technical education. It was decided to set up a Committee of the CABE on "Regulatory Mechanisms for Textbooks and Parallel Textbooks Taught in Schools outside the Government System". The Committee had ten members including two chairpersons, namely Prof. Zoya Hassan and Prof. Gopal Guru. Prof. Krishna Kumar Director, NCERT was the Member-Secretary. The terms of reference of the Committee were:

(a) To study and report on textbooks in government schools not using the CBSE syllabus.
(b) To study the textbooks and curriculum of schools outside the Government system, including those run by the religious and social organizations.
(c) To suggest an appropriate regulatory mechanism for institutionalizing the issue of preparation of textbooks and curricular material.

The CBSE Committee surveyed the present mechanism, a brief of which is presented here in the beginning of this chapter and gave recommendations for developing an appropriate regulatory mechanism for institutionalising the issue of preparation of textbooks and curricular material.

Recommendations on Regulatory Mechanisms for Textbooks and Parallel Textbooks

1. The state has a duty to provide a meaningful quality education for all as part of its duty to provide school education for all, as part of the latter's fundamental right. It is obvious that textbooks are a fulcrum of any system which seeks to provide quality education. We have now an enormous variety of textbooks in the country and the content analysis undertaken for this report shows that there are many problems with textbooks in use in different types of schools. The provision of textbooks in our

country is largely governed by a laissez faire approach. While the plurality in the textbooks and textual materials so produced is and can be fruitful, it is important that these textbooks have to be informed by the philosophy of liberal, secular and democratic education. They need to keep the Constitution and its provisions in view. It is important that textbooks and textual materials are written and produced within this framework and the country must be satisfied that these processes are transparent.

2. There is an urgent need to set up an institutional facility to keep an eye on textbooks. Research on textbooks is an essential feature of a healthy education system, but in the context of the challenges we face, research must take the form of inquiry into specific problems relating to the quality of textbooks and the values they convey. An institutional structure to perform this task needs to be independent of any organization, which is involved, in textbook preparation. This would imply that the institutional facility we are recommending for exercising vigilance on textbooks cannot be associated with the NCERT at the national level and SCERTs at the state level. The NCERT is a major player in the textbook industry and is likely to remain involved in it in the foreseeable future. Therefore, while NCERT's and the SCERT's role as a research organization must extend to research on textbooks, independent institutional structures need to be set up to exercise vigilance on textbooks published by both government organizations as well as by others. The structure can be called National Textbook Council. The State Governments may be encouraged to set up their own State Textbook Council. Both the National Textbook Council and State Textbook Council should be fully autonomous and representing genuine voices in civil society and the academia so that the monitoring of textbooks can be performed with intellectual rigour, sensitivity and commitment to constitutional values. The primary role of these Councils would be to review the contents of textbooks to ensure compliance with the constitutional values and national policies of education. The National Textbook Council may devise its own procedures for review. Given the fact that ordinary citizens do not have a forum where they can complain about content and quality of textbooks, even though their own children are involved, these Councils may especially respond to complaints received from the public about the quality and value perspective of school textbooks by conducting specific inquiries.

3. CABE may set up a Standing Committee. The Standing Committee will inform CABE from time to time about textbook-related, matters and seek guidance from the National Textbook Council. The Committee will from time to time review and examine standards and relevance of textual materials for the educational enterprise and assess the social content of textbooks and textual materials and examine whether they are consistent with the vision of the Constitution and the values of the national policy of education and in terms appropriate for children at different stages of development. It will submit its report to the government and this should be made public.
4. It is extremely important that the principle of periodic review of textual materials be accepted and review undertaken on a regular basis. The CABE Standing Committee can decide the periodicity of such review.
5. Guidelines should be laid down for the periodic review of textual materials of all kinds so that Textbooks are consistent with the secular fabric of Indian governance. Standing Committee would be empowered to prepare the guidelines and outline the parameters for review. It is important that the criteria for approval of textual materials must include a proper analysis of content to assess its adherence to the core principles before the textbooks are approved and prescribed. These will need to be conducted by academic experts who can judge departures from core principles of egalitarianism, democracy, secularism and removal of social barriers, which define the national endeavour of education for all and nation building. These guidelines must be strictly adhered to.
6. The Standing Committee should make these periodic reviews and reports public. It should be widely publicized through the media and other means to increase public awareness of the social content of textbooks and the importance of using textual materials that are in keeping with the values and spirit of egalitarianism, secularism and democracy.
7. The review process must be initiated without inconveniencing parents and children and completed within six months of the beginning of the new academic session.
8. It is a matter of concern that NCERT and SCERTs have so far not taken up research on textbooks as a major area of research and this needs to be strengthened. The NCERT and SCERTs can be asked to set up units dedicated to research on textbook preparation and evaluation. Academic autonomy required for

undertaking this function in an objective manner should be provided to the NCERT and SCERTs.

9. Adequate funding must be made available to concerned agencies for engagning in research on social content of textbooks. Adequate staff must be provided so that it could function in conjunction with and provide support to the CABE standing Committee for curriculum review. The MHRD, State Education Departments and State Directorates of Education should earmark funds for this purpose and all institutions of higher learning should support research in school textbooks.

APPENDIX I

'LEARNING WITHOUT BURDEN (1993) AND RECOMMENDATIONS ON IT BY THE GROUP APPOINTED BY MHRD

Introduction

From time to time a great concern regarding academic burden on students and unsatisfactory quality of learning has bee voiced in our country. The issue came to light when in 1975, the 10+2 pattern of education was introduced. Since then the question has been discussed extensively by several committees and groups. The Ishwar Patel Review Committee (1977), NCERT Working Group (1984) and the Ramamurty Review Committee (1990) on National Policy on Education, 1986 made several recommendations.

With a view to have a fresh look on this problem, the Ministry of Human Resource Development, Government of India appointed a National Advisory Committee in March 1992. The Committee was headed by Prof. Yash Pal, former chairman University Grants Commission and included 7 other members. The Committee gave its recommendation in July 1993.[1]

Terms of Reference of the Committee—The terms of reference were:

"To advice on the ways and means to refuse the load on school students at all levels, particularly the young students, while improved quality of learning including capability for life-long self-learning and skill formulation.

The report of the Committee is entitled '*Learning without Burden.*'

On receipt of the Report of the National Advisory Committee, the Ministry of Human Resource Development set up a group under the Chairmanship of Shri. Y.N. Chaturvedi, Additional Secretary, Department of Education, under the Ministry, the examine the recommendations of the Committee, gave its views on the feasibility of implementing them and a time schedule of implementation. The Committee consisted of 10 members.[2]

---

1. Report of the National Advisory Committee (Yash Pal Committee)
2. Report of the Group of the Ministery of Human Resource Development (Chaturvedi Report)
   Department of Education, M.H.R.D., government of Indian, New Delhi. 1993. Each recommendation of the Committee is followed by the comments of the group.

Recommendation No. 1

A number of organisations and departments organise competitions at district, state and national level for students in various fields such as school subjects, exhibitions, essay writing, elocution, etc. perhaps, the spirit behind these activities is to recognise and reward the talent in diverse fields. But, unfortunately this tends to produce somewhat unheal singling out of people for their brief moment of glory. Competitions where individual achievement is rewarded need to be discouraged since they deprive children of joyful learning. However, group activities and group achievements must be encouraged and rewarded to give a boost to cooperative learning in schools.

Comments

The Group is of the view that group activity and individual effort are not mutually exclusive or antagonistic. rewarding individual achievement does not take away to joy of learning and is also a means to motivate towards higher achievement. In the view of the Group, the educational system should promote performance of the students both as an individual and as a member of the group.

Recommendation No. 2(a)

The process of curriculum framing and preparation of textbooks by decentralised so as to increase teachers' involvement in these tasks. Decentralistion should mean greater autonomy, within state-level apparatus, to district-level boards or other relevant authority, and to heads of school and classroom teachers to develop curricular materials on their own, best suited to needs of local environment. All the schools be encouraged to innovate in all aspects of curriculum, including choice of textbooks and other materials.

Comments

The Group noted that the curriculum and syllabi are designed by the NCERT/CBSE at national level and by the State Boards of Secondary Education/SCERTs at state level by involving teachers and through teachers. However, the number of teachers associated with this exercise is limited to the number of members of the Committee or the Board. The Yash Pal Committee has rightly underlined the need to increase teachers' participation in curriculum development. The Group feels that while the size of committees at national or state level cannot be increased beyond a limit, a meaningful way of improving teachers' participation would be for either the NCERT/CBSE/State Boards/SCERTs to prepare the draft syllabus and finalise it after subjecting it to regional or district level consideration by a large body of teachers or, in the alternative, to get multiple syllabi developed at regional and district levels on the basis of which the final syllabi could be prepared at the state/national level. The Group, however, does not recommend decentralisation in the preparation of syllabus or textbooks at the district or school level because it will be difficult to ensure adequate projection of national identity and of composite culture of India. Also, in such a situation, the adherence to even minimum standards in all parts of the country may become difficult.

In regard to textbooks, the Group agrees with the Yash Pal Committee that the primary responsibility for preparing textbooks, particularly for the lower classes should be that of teachers. It may, however, be remembered that the involvement of experts since the early 1960s led to qualitative improvement in school textbooks. They helped in weeding out dead wood, brought in new perspectives in tune with contemporary knowledge. The Group, however, shares the concern of the Yash Pal Committee that many textbooks presently tend to project predominantly the urban middle class life style. Therefore, the Group recommends that:

(a) The writing of textbooks, as far as possible, should be assigned to school teachers and to those who have developed professional expertise in the area. Subject-matter specialists should be engaged as consultants or advisers to vet the content and presentation of the subject-matter to ensure its accuracy.
(b) In states which have distinct socio-cultural geographical zones, different and parallel sets of textbooks with the same learning objectives should be prepared and used in schools for each such distinct socio-cultural geographical region.
(c) A conscious effort should be made by the textbook preparation agencies to take examples from rural areas for illustrating various points became a large majority of students are in rural areas.
(d) The text-books preparation agencies should undertake systematic review of all textbooks in a time-bound manner to ensure that any trivial matter which may have got included in the textbooks is weeded out. Similarly, such a review should also try to eliminate elements of repetitions of the topics covered in previous classes.
(e) The Group noted that, in some cases, the textbooks for subjects other than languages in some classes are written in a language which is considerably more complex and difficult than the language used in textbooks for that class. It, therefore, recommends that the group which writes a textbook should

include one language teacher who should vet the manuscript to ensure that the degree of difficulty of the language used in the subject-matter is not more than the degree of difficulty designed for language competency for that class. It regard to curriculum transaction and teaching materials, the Group noted that there are no restrictions and teaching materials, the Group noted that there are no restrictions on schools and teachers to innovate. Indeed, the teacher training courses have consistently advocated this and many organisations have introduced special programmes to promote this. Needless, to say that school and teachers should be motivated to innovate to the fullest extent in regard to teaching methods and use of teaching materials.

Recommendation No. 2(b)

Voluntary organisations with a specific commitment to pedagogical innovations within the formal or non-formal system be provided greater freedom and support in development of curriculum, textbooks and teacher training. A suitable and adequate mechanism be evolved for wider dissemination of the experiences of such organisation.

Comments

The Group fully agrees that voluntary organisation with a commitment to education should be encouraged in all possible manners. The Group also noted that the governments, both at the national and the state levels have, in recent past, made a substantial move to expand such cooperation. The process needs to be continued. However, for reason mentioned in 2(a), the Group does not favour decentralisation in curriculum development and textbooks preparation to the extent of entrusting it to voluntary organisation because of the sensitivity of the matter.

Recommendation No. 2(c)

We ensure the idea of setting up education at village, block and district levels to undertake planning and supervision of schools under their jurisdiction.

Comments

This is acceptable in principle. This has been strongly advocated in para 10.8 of the NPE, 1986. Following the Constitutional Amendment for decentralisation at Panchayat level, the Central Advisory Board of Education (CABE) has already constituted a Committee on Decentralised Management of Education to examine and recommend measures for effectively carrying out the desired involvement of the local committees.

Therefore, this recommendation should be implemented in the light of the recommendations of the CABE Committee.

Recommendation No. 2(d)

Sufficient contingency amount (not less than 10 per cent of the total salary bill of the school) be placed at the disposal of heads of schools for purchase, repair and replacement of pedagogical equipment.

Comments

This is acceptable. The State/UT Governments and autonomous bodies of the Central Government controlling their respective chain of schools (Kendriya Vidyalayas, Navodaya Vidyalayas, Central Tibetan Schools, Railway Schools and Sainik Schools and other schools run by the Defence establishments) should be urged to give this authority to the Principals/ Headmasters of the schools to make repairs to school buildings, purchase, repair and replace pedagogical equipment and books and also to carry out innovative projects, subject to the control of the local education committees. The organisations controlling the schools and the State Governments should categorically specify that the Head of the school does not require approval should categorically specify that the Head of the school does not require approval of any higher educational authority and the School management/Advisory Committee for using the available money for these purposes.

Recommendation No. 3

The culture of writing textbooks be changes so as to involve a much larger number of teachers in the preparation of textbooks. The scientists and experts in various disciplines may be associated with the preparation of textbooks as consultants and not as writers of the books. Initiative in this regard should rest with groups of enlightened and innovative teachers who should be provided training in book writing

Comments

The group agrees with the purpose of this recommendation—greater involvement of teachers—and the views of the Group this recommendations included in the comments on 2(a).

Recommendation No. 4

At least three parallel systems of school education (syllabus, textbooks and examination) are running concurrently in different states. In each state majority of schools are affiliated to the State Board of Education while a few are affiliated to either CBSE or ICSE. The schools affiliated to CBSE in the states other than Delhi enjoy the prestige of being elite schools. The CBSE curriculum becomes a trend-setter for the State Boards leading to heavier curriculum for majority of children. Therefore, the Committee recommends that jurisdiction of CBSE be restricted to Kendriya and Navodayas and all other schools be affiliated to the respective State Boards.

Comments

The Group has been unable to appreciate the arguments put forth by the Yash Pal Committee in this recommendation. The choice of education boards that the schools have is already very limited—there is no free choice—and it can be exercised only with the approval of the State Government. Therefore, if a school in any part of the country had the choice of affiliating with one Board or the other, it should be generally good for education. As for CBSE, it relies heavily on the NCERT for developing syllabi and preparing textbooks. The NCERT, in turn, operates within the national policy framework and on the basis of guidelines contained in the National Curriculum Framework. Rightly the NCERT keeps in view the existing standards in the country, the capability of students, and standards in developed countries because the syllabus and textbook must take note of all these. If there is unnecessary material in some of the NCERT books, it should be eliminated as the Group has suggested in the preceding recommendations. However, there is not adequate material on record to substantiate that CBSE syllabi or NCERT books *per se* are overloaded. Also, the Yash Pal Committee has recommended that affiliation to CBSE should restricted to Kendriya and Navodaya Vidyalas, with all other schools being affiliated to respective State Boards. If affiliation to the CBSE is good for Kendriya and Navodya Vidyalayas it cannot be bad for other schools.

Recommendation No. 5(a)

Appropriate legislative and administrative measures be adopted to regulate the opening and functioning of early childhood education institutions (pre-schools). Norms regarding accommodation, staff, apparatuses, play materials be laid down for the recognition of these schools. It should be ensured that these institutions do not perpetrate violence on young children by inflicting a heavy dose of 'over education' in the form of formal teaching of Reading, Writing and Numbers. The practice of holding tests and interviews for admission to nursery class be abolished.

Recommendation No. 5(b)

Norms for granting recognition to private schools be made more stringent. This will prove conducive for improving the quality of learning on one hand and arrest growing commercialisation on the other. The norms, thus developed, be made uniformly applicable to all schools including he state run institutions.

Comments [5(a) and 5(b)]

The Group is in agreement with the recommendations. While the NCERT has prepared some norms for the staff, nature of curriculum and educational material for pre-primary stage, this sector of education in the country is largely unsupervised and unregulated. It is also a known fact that most of these schools are loading the students with the burden of formal teaching of various subjects. The Group advised that an appropriate regulatory mechanism should be urgently set up in the country to ensure that learning at this stage is by playway method and formal teaching of subjects is scrupulously prevented. Similarly the Group agrees that recognition and affiliation of both private and government schools should be made more stringent so that schools lacking in minimum essential facilities are not allowed to function because it really means punishment to the students. Although there is a well set arrangement for recognition and affiliation of schools but due to extraneous pressures the standards sometimes are not observed. The Group would like to suggest that the possibility of having a legislation to specify norms of facilities in schools and providing for powers to prevent opening of schools which do not have facilities should be seriously considered.

Recommendation No. 6

There is no justification for torturing the young children compelling them to carry heavy bags of books everyday to schools. Textbooks should be treated as school property and thus, there should be no need for children to purchase the books individually and carry them daily to homes. A separate time-table for the assignment of homework and for the use of textbooks and notebooks be prepared by the school and be made known to the children in advance.

Recommendation No. 7

The nature and character of homework needs a radical change. In the primary classes, children should not be given any homework, save for extension of explorations in the home environment. In the upper primary and secondary classes, homework, where necessary; should be non-textual, and textbooks, when needed for work at home should be made available on a rotation basis.

Comments (6 and 7)

The Group has already agreed that there should be no formal teaching of subjects in the pre-school stages. The Group also feels that there should be no homework and project work at the primary stage (Classes I-V). However, it is an extreme point of observation that textbooks should be treated as school property. Besides the financial implications arising out of the burden on schools to purchase the textbooks and the concomitant responsibility on the schools to store the books when most of the schools of the country do not have either the financial resources or storage capacities, the children would be devoid of the opportunity to refer to the textbooks in their homes. For an overwhelming majority of school students of the country, the textbooks remain as the only source of reading material. The Group recommends that the class routine for the upper primary, secondary and higher secondary stages should be drawn up in such a way that every subject is not required to be taught everyday. This should be included in the norms for compliance by every school which the Group has suggested in para 5(a) and (5(b) above.

Recommendation No. 8

The existing norms for teacher-pupil ratio (i.e. 1:40) should be enforced and an attempt should be made to reduce this to 1:30, at least in the primary classes, as a basis for future educational planning.

Comments

The Group agrees with a higher teacher-pupil ratio with improved teaching and standards of education. It understands that in reality the existing teacher-pupil ratio is around 1:40 in most parts of the country. Attempts should be made to bring it to 1:30 over a period of time. Such change in ratio would have a very large financial implication because of the need to induct a large number of extra teachers and, therefore, this can be done only over a period of time. Efforts should be made to ensue that the class size does exceed 40.

Recommendation No. 9

Greater use of the electronic media be made for the creation of a child-centred social ethos in the country. A regular television program addressed to students, teachers and parents and possibly called 'Shiksha Darshan' be launched, along the lines of the 'Krishi Darshan' programme.

Comments

Greater use of electronic media for education is an essential part of modernising the educational system. A regular programme on TV addressed to students, teachers and parents would be welcome. The Group took note of the fact that the Ministry of Human Resource Development, department of Education, has already made a request for allocating one channel for education out of 15 or 16 channels which have recently become available with the commissioning of INSAT 2-A. The Group strongly suggests that an educational channel should be operationalised at the earliest and this channel should include a programme of the nature suggested by the Yash Pal Committee.

Recommendation No. 10(a)

Inadequate programme of teacher preparation leads to unsatisfactory quality of learning in schools. The B.Ed. programme should offer the possibility of specialisation in secondary or elementary or nursery education. The duration of the programme should either be one year after graduation or three-four years after higher secondary. The content of the programme should be restructured to ensure its relevance to the changing needs of school education and to make it more practicum-centred. The emphasis in these programmes should be on enabling the trainees to acquire the ability of self-learning and independent thinking. Pre-service teacher education programme, being a professional course, has to be a rigorous, thorough and intensive programme. Therefore, B.Ed. degree courses by correspondence be de-recognised.

Comments

There is a lot of merit in the argument advanced by the Yash Pal Committee for having a programme of B.Ed. aimed at elementary or secondary education. In metropolitan cities, a large number of teachers are actually getting recruited for pre-school and elementary schools with B.Ed. qualifications. Recruitment of KVS and NVS is also, in practice, based on B.Ed. qualifications. Recruitment in KVS and NVS is also, in practice, based on B.Ed. qualifications. Therefore, this reality needs to be taken cognizance of and the present practice of focussing on secondary education in B.Ed. needs to be given up by enabling B.Ed. to be pursued with either specialisation in secondary or in elementary or in pre-school education. In any case the existing arrangements, including the District Institutes of Education and Training (DIETs) for preparing primary school teachers need to be continued and strengthened.

The recommendation of the Yash Pal Committee for de-recognising

B.Ed. degree by correspondence course is more problematic, while the National Council for Teacher Education (NCTE) has earlier made recommendations on these lines and the UGC has been interacting with the concerned universities during the last ten years on that basis, such courses are continuing. A recent expert committee of the UGC has expressed that for women candidates and for people from rural areas, B.Ed. correspondence course opens up valuable career opportunities. Also, in a large number of countries, B.Ed. through correspondence course is one of the prominent courses in distance mode. These arguments cannot be totally ignored. The Group understands that the matter is at an advanced stage of consideration in the UGC. Also the NCTE as a statutory body is expected to become operational in the near future. The Group recommends that this matter should be referred to the UGC and the NCTE for appropriate decision.

Recommendation No. 10(b)

The continuing education of teachers must be institutionalised. The organisation of inservice education programmes and other activities aimed at professional growth of teachers be systematically designed and conducted imaginatively.

Comments

The emphasis given by the Yash Pal Committee to continuing education of teachers is totally unexceptionable. Thus, DIET's are being set up in the country primarily to meet this need. Distance education system also is coming up in the country which can be used to meet the needs of inservice education. However, the progress in this regard has been slow. The Group fully endorses the need to set up arrangements for regular and periodic in-service training of teachers and recommends that the DIET's should be operationalised as early as possible and the distance mode of education should be used extensively to strengthen in-service training of teachers.

Recommendation No. 11

The public examinations taken at the end of Class X and XII be reviewed with a view to ensure replacement of the prevailing text-based and 'quiz type' questioning by the concept-based questioning. This single reform is sufficient to improve the quality of learning and save the children from the tyranny of rote memorisation.

Comments

The Group feels that the Yash Pal Committee's reference to the concept-based questioning perhaps advocates greater importance to questions of higher ability. The Group agrees with this but it should be remembered that assessment should test various kinds of abilities and not just one kind. The Group also feels that the Boards of School Education should emphasise Continuous and Comprehensive Evaluation (CCE) that incorporates both scholastic and non-scholastic aspects of education, spread over the total span of instructional time as stipulated in para 8.24 (iii) of the NPE, 1986.

Recommendation No. 12(a)

A project team with a number of sub-groups be set up in each state to examine the syllabi and textbooks for all school classes. The sub-groups be required to decide the following:

(i) The minimum number of topics required to be taught.
(ii) The minimum number of concepts to be introduced within each topic.
(iii) The total time needed for teaching this minimum number of concepts comfortably by a teacher in the total working days realistically available in a year.

Comments

The Minimum Levels of Learning (MLLs) for language (mother tongue), mathematics and environmental studies for Classes I-V have already been prepared at the national level in 1990 and the NCERT, the Boards of School Education and the SCERTs have developed their resources to introduce the MLLs at the primary stage. Therefore, setting up another Project Team for the same purpose would amount to avoidable duplication. The Group feels that though in para 5.4.5(vii) and para 21.3.1 (a), the POA, 1992 has called for laying down MLLs at the upper primary stage and in para 21.3.1 (b), the POA, 1992 has urged the Boards to lay down expected levels of attainment at Classes IX-XII, the reasonableness of laying down MLLs at the upper primary stage and above deserves a careful reconsideration since knowledge base in supposed to grow at a fast pace after the primary stage. Moreover, with emphasis shifting to subject-matter learning at the upper stage and above, the idea of laying down uniform MLLs after primary stage does not seem to be a viable proposition. However, at the time of curriculum renewal and preparation of textbooks, the curriculum/textbook designers should systematically check that those can be covered within the instructional time available to teachers. The NCERT at the national level and the State Boards/SCERTs/ SIEs at the state level may consider the desirability of reviewing the school curricula/textbooks to ensure that non-essential matter and repetitive treatment of concepts in subjects in different classes is minimised as far as possible without sacrificing the requirements of cognitive development.

Recommendation No. 12(b)

Mathematics curriculum for primary classes in all parts of the country be reviewed with a view to slowing down the pace at which children are required to learn basic mathematical concepts, and broadening the scope of primary mathematics to include areas other than number work (e.g. space-and shape-related concepts and problem solving). The tendency embedded in the syllabi and textbooks of primary mathematics to accelerate children's mathematical skills by teaching them mechanical rules at the expense of understanding and intelligent application ought to be discouraged in future syllabi and texts.

Comments

The Group endorses the recommendation that mathematics and syllabi for other subjects should be reviewed to assess whether they are overloaded. But it would not like to state at this stage that they indeed are overloaded. The MLLs adopted by the MHRD are now being tried out and the question of review should be considered only on the basis of the feedback. As has been referred to in the preceding recommendations syllabi have to be designed keeping in view the existing standards, and capacity of students and standards in developed countries. However, the Group endorses the statement of the Yash Pal Committee that the syllabus should emphasise understanding and intelligent application rather than memorising without understanding.

Recommendation No. 12(c)

Language textbooks should adequately reflect the spoken idiom. An attempt should be made in future textbooks to give adequate representation to children's life experiences, imaginary stories and poems, and stories reflecting the lives of ordinary people in different parts of the country. Pedantic language and excessive didacticism ought to be avoided.

Comments

These recommendations are acceptable. The NCERT and the Boards including CBSE and Council for the Indian School Certificate Examination (CISCE) should review their respective language textbooks from these angles.

Recommendation No. 12(d)

Science syllabi and textbooks in the primary classes should provide greater room and necessity for experimentation than they do at present. In place of didacticism in areas like health and sanitation, the texts should emphasise analytical reflection on real-life situation. A great deal of trivial material included in primary-level science texts should be dropped.

Comments

The Group has already given its views that all the existing textbooks should be screened in a time-bound manner for eliminating trivial matter and repetition. The Group endorses the recommendation that there should be greater scope for experimentation at the primary stage. This should be systematically promoted through a large programme of in-service education of teachers.

Recommendation No. 12(e)

The syllabi of natural sciences throughout the secondary and senior secondary classes be revised in a manner so as to ensure that most of the topics included are actively linked to experiments or activities that can be performed by children and teachers.

Comments

The Group is of the view that while experiments and activities at all levels are important, the selection of topics in science curriculum at higher stages cannot be determined by the criterion that they are linked to experiment, etc. Every effort should, however, be made to see that experiments and activities, as much as possible, depending on the nature of the topic, are made a part of science teaching even at higher levels.

Recommendation No. 12(f)

Besides imparting knowledge of history and geography the social sciences curriculum for classes VI-VIII and IX-X should convey the philosophy and methodology of the functions of our socio-political and economic system and enable the students to analyse, understand and reflect on the problems and priorities of socio-economic development. The repetitions nature of history syllabus should be changed. The history of ancient times should be introduced for systematic study in secondary classes (IX and X). The history syllabus for classes VI-VIII should focus on the freedom struggle and post-independence developments. The civics, as it is taught today, puts a great load on children's capacity to memorise. Therefore, it may be dropped in its present form and be replaced by contemporary studies. The study of geography be related to contemporary reality.

Comments

As regards the Committee's suggestion that history syllabus for classes VI-VIII should focus on freedom struggle and post-independence developments, the Group holds the view that a large majority of children drop out at the end of class VIII, which is also the last year of compulsory education and, therefore, it would not be educationally sound to allow such a big section of our children to remain oblivious of the entire heritage of India before the freedom struggle. The Committee seems to have linked spiral approach (which is based on a well-established principle of curriculum construction) with repetition which leads to boredom and load and trivialisation of ideas. The Group feels that is geography greater importance should be given to the study of contemporary problems. The context or implications of the Committee's recommendation for replacing 'Civics' by 'Contemporary Studies' are not clear.

Additional Suggestions for the Group

The Yash Pal Committee has made many thought-provoking recommendations which the Group has tried to recommend for implementation in a more specific manner. If these are implemented efficiently, the standards of school education will undoubtedly improve and as the Yash Pal Committee has envisaged alienation of students from education and the burden of non-understanding on them would effectively diminish. However, in addition to the recommendations made by the Yash Pal Committee, there are a few more issues which immediately present themselves for consideration while considering any exercises for reducing the load of curriculum. The Group would like to suggest these also for implementation.

1. Age of Entry

It is a known fact that in India children join school at a rather early age than their counterparts do in most of the developed countries. At the age of 4 and 5, a different of one year in age makes a lot of difference in the mental capability of a child. A more mature child can easily cope with the learning requirements. The effect early admissions of children in schools, particularly at the pre-primary stage, is that she/he is unable to cope with the demands that the syllabus makes and consequently she/he starts in a situation of personal inadequacy. This contributed significantly to the loads of non-learning. It is, therefore, desirable that the minimum age of admission to pre-primary classes and in primary classes should be reconsidered for being raised by one year.

2. Teaching Days

Kothari Commission recommended 210 teaching days but the actual number of school days are 125-150. Since the syllabi are framed on the basis that 210 days will be available, this only means that either a part of syllabus is not covered by the teacher or that she/he covers the syllabus in a hurried manner which creates difficulty for students for being able to cope with a lot of content in a limited time. Effective action to increase the number of teaching days to 210 in a year would undoubtedly very substantially reduce the daily learning load and would also improve standards.

3. Classroom Facilities

In large number of schools in the country not only the facilities in the classroom but the classroom themselves are grossly deficient. This inevitably affects the quality of teaching and, therefore, of learning. The Yash Pal Committee has recommended and we have endorsed that recommendation earlier in this Report that norms for school facilities should be effectively and strictly enforced for recognition/affiliation. However, since government is the major funding agency for most school, there should be positive movement for improving availability of classrooms and improving availability of educational aids in schools. For primary schools, the Government of India is implementing a large programme of Operation Blackboard and in the Eighth Plan it is being extended to cover upper primary classes also. At secondary level, the government of India is implementing a scheme for assisting schools for improving science equipment. However, a much large effort needs to be made. It would be imperative that the effort of the government is supplemented by individuals and philanthropic bodies because the requirement is large. It would be appropriate that the governments and the school systems consider how best they can encourage such individuals and philanthropic bodies to help schools to develop.

4. Strengthening of the Professional Support System

An area which needs to be looked into is the qualitative improvement of professional bodies like the SCERTs, Textbook Bureaus and Boards of School Education who are primarily responsible for curriculum, textbooks and examinations. It is these bodies which will ultimately have to reckon with the problem of load. Under the centrally sponsored scheme of teacher education, there is a component of strengthening of SCERTs which should be taken up a priority basis.

5. "...impact of examinations, admission to higher educational institutions, including professional courses"

This was one of the terms of reference of the Committee which has not been dealt with in the Report. The CABE may consider to refer this matter to a committee drawn from school and higher education. Another term of reference of the Committee related to "the measures such as formal recognition and weightage to sports and games and co-curricular and extra-curricular activities..." A CABE Committee is looking into this matter and its report is expected to be presented to the CABE shortly.

Time Schedule for Implementation

As regards laying down a time schedule for implementation of the recommendations found feasible the Group felt that the recommendations are of long-term nature. Moreover, the report of the National Advisory Committee as well as this report of the Group would be placed before the CABE in its meeting scheduled to be held on 15-10-1993. As such, it would be advisable to wait for CABE's approved to Committee's recommendations and then draw up a time schedule for implementation of the recommendations accepted by the CABE.

APPENDIX 2

CENTRAL ADVISORY BOARD OF EDUCATION (CABE): ITS FUNCTIONS AND CONSTITUTION

Resolution

1. The Central Advisory Board of Education (CABE), the highest advisory body to advise the Central and State Governments in the field of education, was first established in 1920 and dissolved in 1923 as a measure of economy. It was revived in 1935 and had continued to be in existence till 1994. Despite the fact that in the past, important decisions had been taken on the advice of CABE and it had provided a forum for widespread consultation and examination of issues relating to educational and cultural development, it was unfortunately not reconstituted after the expiry of its extended tenure in March, 1994. CABE has a particularly important role to play at the present juncture in view of the significant socio-economic and socio-cultural developments taking place in the country and for the review of the national Policy on Education which is also due. It is a matter of importance therefore, that the Central and State Governments, and educationists and people representing all interests, should increase their interaction and evolve a participative process of decision making in education, which enhances the federal structure of our polity.
2. The Government of India has accordingly decided to reconstitute CABE as per the annexure.
3. The functions of CABE would be:
   (a) to review the progress of education from time to time;
   (b) to appraise the extent and manner in which the education policy has been implemented by the Central and State Governments, and other concerned agencies, and to give appropriate advice in the matter.
   (c) to advise regarding coordination between the Central and State Governments/UT Administrations, State Governments and non-governmental agencies for educational development in accordance with the education policy; and

(d) to advise, suo moto, or on a reference made to it by the Central Government or any State Government or a Union Territory Administration on any educational question.

4. For the discharge of these functions, the Board may:
   (i) call for information and comments from any Government institution, any other organisation or an individual;
   (ii) appoint committees or groups comprising members of CABE and/or others as may be necessary; and
   (iii) commission, through Government or any other agency, studies, research or reports on any specific issue requiring the attention of the Board or its committees or groups.

5. (a) *Tenure*—The tenure of CABE shall be three years, with effect from the date of this notification.

   (b) Casual Vacancies:
      (i) All casual vacancies among the members, other than ex-officio members shall be filled by the authority or body which nominated or elected the member whose place falls vacant.
      (ii) The person nominated or elected to a casual vacancy shall be a member of the Board for the residue of the term for which the member whose place he fills would have been a member.

   (c) *Meeting*—The Board will meet at least once every year and there shall not be a gap of more than two years between two consecutive meetings of the Board.

   (d) *Agenda*—(i) The Agenda, the explanatory memorandum and the record of proceedings/minutes will be prepared and circulated by the Ministry of Human Resource Development (Department of Secondary and Higher Education), Government of India (ii) The Agenda and the explanatory memorandum will ordinarily be circulated to all the members at least 15 days before the date of the meeting of the Board.

   (e) *Quorum*—The quorum of the meeting of the Board will be 2/3rd of the total membership of the Board.

   (f) *Procedure*—The Board will adopt its own procedures in respect of matters not provided for above.

   (g) *General*—No proceedings of the Board shall be invalid merely on the ground of procedural defect or vacancy under any category of membership.

Sd/-

C. Balakrishnan

Joint Secretary to the Government of India

Order

Ordered that a copy of the Resolution be published in the Gazette of India for general information. Also ordered that a copy of the Resolution be forwarded to all the Ministries/Departments of the Government of India, all State Governments/Union Territories Administration, Universities, Institutions/Organisations of the Department of Secondary and Higher Education, Ministry of Human Resource Development etc. for information. (F. No. 2-24/93-PN.I)

Sd/-
C. Balakrishnan
Joint Secretary to the Government of India

To

The Manager,
Government of India Press
Faridabad

Copy forwarded to:

1. All Members of CABE.
2. All Permanent Invitees.
3. All Ministries/Departments of the Government of India.
4. All Attached/Subordinate Offices and Autonomous Statutory Bodies under the Ministry of Human Resource Development.
5. All State Governments/Union Territories.
6. President's Secretariat.
7. Prime Minister's Office.
8. Cabinet Secretariat.
9. Lok Sabha Secretariat.

Sd/-
C. Balakrishnan
Joint Secretary to the Government of India

Annexure

Composition of the Central Advisory Board of Education:

1. Chairman, Minister of Human Resource Development.
2. Vice-Chairman, Minister of State for Human Resource Development.
3. Representatives of the Government of India
   (i) Minister of Information and Broadcasting.
   (ii) Minister of Science and Technology.
   (iii) Minister of health and Family Welfare.

(iv) Minister of Labour.
(v) Minister of Social Justice and Empowerment.
(vi) Minister of Tribal Affairs.
(vii) Minister of Youth Affairs and Sports.
(viii) Member (Education), Planning Commission.

4. Representatives of State Governments and UT Administrations:
(i) One Minister in charge of Education in each State Government (to be nominated by the Chief Minister).
(ii) Lt. Governor or Minister in-charge of Education in each UT Administration.

5. Elected Members
(i) Four Members of Parliament from the Lok Sabha.
(ii) Two Members of Parliament from the Rajya Sabha.

6. Ex-officio Members
(i) Secretary, Department of Elementary Education and Literacy, Government of India.
(ii) Chairman, University Grants Commission.
(iii) Chairman, All India Council for Technical Education.
(iv) Chairman, Central Council of Indian Medicine.
(v) Chairman, Central Council of Indian Medicine.
(vi) Director General, Indian Council of Agricultural Research.
(vii) Chairman, Central Social Welfare Board.
(viii) Director, National Institute of Educational Planning and Administration.
(ix) Director, National Council for Educational, Research and Training.
(x) Chairman, Central Board of Secondary Education.
(xi) Secretary-General, Association of Indian Universities.
(xii) Chairman, Indian Council of Historical Research.
(xiii) Chairman, Indian Council for Social Science Research.
(xiv) Chairman, Indian Council for Philosophical Research.
(xv) Director-General, National Literacy Mission.

7. Nominated Members—representing different interests (in alphabetical order)
   1. Shri Javed Akhtar,
      702, Sagar Samrat, Green Field,
      Juhu, Bombay-400049.
   2. Shri U.R. Anandamurthy,
      498 Suragi, HIG House, RMV IInd Stage,
      6th A Main, Bangalore-560094.

3. Prof. Andre Beteille, Sociologist,
   69, Jor Bagh, (Ground Floor), New Delhi-03.
4. Ms. Ela Bhatt, General Secretary,
   SEWA, Opp. Victoria Garden,
   Bhadra, Ahmdabad-380001.
5. Shri Praful Bidwai,
   1st Floor, Anand Villa, 1 Jaipur Estate,
   Nizamuddin East, New Delhi-110003.
6. Shri Charles Correa,
   Charles Correa Associates,
   9 Mathew Roa, Bombay-400004.
7. Ms. G. Nirmala Deshpande,
   A 223 Pandara Road, New Delhi.
8. Shri G.P. Deshpande,
   10B, Athashree, Pashan, Sus Road,
   Pashan, Pune.
9. Ms. Mahashweta Devi,
   50B, Prince Gulam Saha Road,
   Ground Floor, Calcutta 700 032.
10. Shri Jean Dreze,
    Centre for Dev. Economics,
    Dept. of Economics, Delhi School of Economics,
    University of Delhi-110007
11. Shri S.V. Giri, VC,
    S.S. Institute of Higher Learning,
    Prashanti Nilayam, Anantapur 515134.
12. Prof. J.S. Grewal,
    29 Sector 11, Chandigarh-180016.
13. Shri Gopal Guru,
    90, New Transit Hostel, Phase-III,
    JNU Campus, New Delhi.
14. Ms. Zoya Hasan,
    139 Uttra Khand, Jawaharlal Nehru University,
    New Delhi-110057
15. Prof. P.V. Indiresan,
    B-57, Hill View Apartments,
    Vasant Vihar, New Delhi-110057.
16. Shri J.J. Irani
    Bombay House,
    24, Homi Modi Street, Fort, Mumai-40001.
17. Shri Kiran Karnik,
    Chairman, NASSCOM,

International Youth Centre, Teen Murti Marg,
Chanakyapuri, New Delhi-110021.

18. Ms. Kiran Shaw Mazumdar,
Chairperson, BIOCON India Ltd.,
20th KM Hosur Road, Electronic City,
Bangalore-560100.

19. Prof. Mrinal Miri,
Vice-Chancellor North Eastern Hill University,
NEHU Campus, Shillong, Meghalaya-793002.

20. Ms. Shubha Mudgal,
39B, MIG Flats, Matia Khan,
Paharganj, New Delhi.

21. Dr. Jayant Narlikar,
Inter-University Centre for Astronomy & Astrophysics
Post Bag 4,
Ganeshkshind, Pune-411007.

22. Shri Sandeep Pande, Co-Ordinator, Asha (Hope)-Lalpur,
A-893, Indira Nagar, Lucknow-226016.

23. Shri Azim Premji,
Chairman, Wipro, Doddakannelli Sarjapur Road,
Bangalore-560035.

24. Shri Vinod Raina,
Chair Arena Council of Fellows,
E1/193, ARERA Colony, Bhopal-462 016.

25. Shri Anil Sadagopal,
Professor of Education, University of Delhi,
E-13 Kalindi, New Delhi-110065.

26. Ms. Teesta Seetalvad,
Editor, Communalism Combat,
Sabrang Communications Pvt. Ltd.,
P.B. No. 28253, Juhu Post Office,
Juhu, Mumbai-400049.

27. Shri Kiran Seth,
Associate Professor,
Production & Industrial Engg., IIT, Delhi.

28. Ms. Kumud Sharma,
F-9-G, Munirka DDA Flats, New Delhi.
29. Shri P B Sharma,
Principal, Delhi College of Engineering,
Bawana Road, Delhi 110042.

30. Ms. Shanta Sinha, Secretary,
C/o M. Venkatarangaiya Foundation,

28, West Maredpalli, Road No. 1,
Secundrabad-500026.

31. Ms. Krishna Sobti,
505-B, Purvasha, Anand Lok Housing Society,
Mayur Vihar, Phase-I, New Delhi-110091.

8. **Member Secretary**

Secretary, Department of Secondary and Higher Education, Ministry of Human Resource Development, Government of India.

9. **Permanent Invitees**

(i) Secretary, Department of Women and Child Development.
(ii) Secretary, Department of Youth Affairs and Sports.
(iii) Secretary, Department of Culture.
(iv) Secretary, Department of Science and Technology.
(v) Secretary, Ministry of Social Justice and Empowerment.
(vi) Secretary, Tribal Affairs.
(vii) Secretary, Planning Commission.
(viii) Secretary, Department of Labour.
(ix) Secretary, Department of Industrial Policy and Promotion.
(x) Secretary, Ministry of Information Technology.

APPENDIX 3

QUALITY EDUCATION FOR YOUNG PEOPLE: UNESCO/ICE (2004)

Meeting at the 47th session of the UNESCO International Conference on Education (Geneva, 8-11, September 2004), we, the Ministers of Education, heads of delegation and delegates from 137 Member States have, alongside representatives of 14 intergovernmental organizations, 21 NGOs and foundations, taken part in rich, frank and open debates on the theme *'Quality Education for all Young People Challenges, Trends and Priorities'*. The youth attending the Conference expressed their desire for an education that responds to their expectations and expressed the high hopes that they place in this important event. This theme allowed us to share our concerns and difficulties, to jointly seek perspectives for solutions, to reaffirm our hopes and to reinforce international dialogue on educational policies. Education for All (EFA) goals were at the centre of our efforts and of the commitments made by the international community in Jomtien, Dakar and within the essence reflected in the Millennium Development Declaration and those of the United Nations Decade of Education for Sustainable Development and the International Literacy Decade, to improve the quality of education for all young people. It has become increasingly clear in all parts of the world that basic education can no longer be limited to primary education.

Message

1. Promoting quality education and training for all young people between the ages of 12 and 18/20 is essential to securing a better future and constitutes an essential mechanism for combating social exclusion at the local, national and global levels. As both a basic right and a public good, this education must respond to the needs and interests of all young people with a view to ensuring the realization of their full potential, their successful integration in the world of work, as well as their capacity to participate in active life and as responsible citizens.
2. In particular, this Conference has allowed us to agree at an international level on several fundamental aspects relative to

the construction and reinforcement of our educational policies. There appears to be a need to :

— recognize that while all countries, both in the North and the South, are confronted with difficulties, the situation of the education of youth is particularly dramatic in many developing countries where education systems appear to continue to be insufficiently adapted to the needs both of young people themselves, as well as those of society at large.
— help young people confront an increasingly complex world characterized, in particular, by the challenges of humanizing globalization, by the important role of information and knowledge as factors of production and of development, by the increasing scale of population movements, by the marginalization of many social groups, as well as by the exacerbation of inequalities and poverty both among and within countries.
— continue improving, in more practical and efficient ways, young girls' access to and participation in education.
— ensure that all young people acquire the competencies required for personal autonomy and for citizenship, to enter the world of work and social life, with a view to respecting their identity, openness to the world and social and cultural diversity.
— reinforce—through education for active and responsible citizenship—the willingness and the capacity to live together and to build peace in a world characterized by interstate and internal armed conflicts and by the emergence of all forms of violence and war.
— reaffirm the central role of teaches and trainers and to reinforce their professionalism both through their heightening status, as well as through pre- and in-service training, with a view to better preparing them to handle the new demands placed upon them by young people and society at large.

3. In many countries education systems, often inherited from the past, are no longer able to respond to the challenges that they are confronted with. New, broader and diversified pathways need to be defined. It is becoming increasingly clear that improving the quality of education for all young people can no longer be ensured by the public authorities, teachers and formal education systems alone. Education is the affair of all.

4. Through this Conference, we reaffirm the crucial importance of education for our national development policies. We are consequently making an appeal for the mobilization of all partners, in order to enable ourselves to respond to the immense challenges of the education of young people, globalization with a human face and sustainable development of our societies and of the planet as a whole. Only through new efficient alliances and partnerships can we find diversified and adapted solutions to respond to the present and future needs of young people and to improve the quality of their education. These alliances must be built and reinforced within states themselves, as well as between governments, civil society, the economic sector, the media and youth themselves. they must also be reinforced between development partners at the regional and international levels, so that the commitments undertaken by the international community supporting improvements the quality of education may be met.
5. We also express our hope that the Conclusions and Proposed for Active that we adopted unanimously on 11 September 2004 may become an effective source of information for our educational policies and serve to improve in a effective and sustainable way the quality of education for all young people active the world for peace, justice and sustainable development.

Challenges

6. *Sheer numbers*—At present, half the world's population is under age 25. The world has the largest generation of young people ever. More than I billion people a between the age of 12 and 20. In 2020, 87% of young people in the world will live developing countries, where today they are already the majority. Developed counties will be faced with the demographic challenge of an ever-ageing population.
7. *Greater access and opportunities*—The number of young people comp0leting prim school is constantly rising. The number of enrolments at secondary school level the world has multiplied tenfold over the last 50 years. While secondary school enrolments on a global level increased from 56% to 77.5% in the last decade, their masks the reality that millions of young people, particularly in the south, while finish primary school are still denied the opportunities to maker a living or continue their education. Furthermore, many do not even complete prima education, Females are particularly affected.

8. *Improved quality of education for the twenty-first century*—Too many young people do not have the opportunity to acquire the necessary knowledge, attitudes at values for life in the twenty-first century. There is a demand for education to last relevant to the modern world and to create learners for life. Therefore, the qualification of education for this age group is now at the heart of national and international concerns.
9. *Gender equality*—In most of parts of the world, there are unacceptable gender differences in access, opportunities, retention and learning outcomes. This reflects their inability of many education systems to be gender-responsive.
10. *Competencies for life*—Currently, education systems do not provide young people opportunities to obtain and strengthen the complex set of competencies for life including technical and vocational education. Many of these competencies an essential for addressing modern problems such as HIV/AIDS and other pandemic diseases, exiting and entering the labour force and social and political indifference. Lack of technical and vocational education and training, including entrepreneurial ship and training for creativity, hampers employability.
11. *Social inclusion*—In a world that is increasingly becoming closer due to globalization and information and communication technologies, exclusion is on the increase. Factors such as poverty, gender, ability, origin, language, culture and various kinds of discrimination can impinge on effective learning.
12. *Conducive conditions for teacher*—Teachers and trainers in many parts of the world lack sufficient training, resources, support, materials and conducive conditions of service. As a result they cannot be effective in facilitating the learning of young people.
13. *Anticipating the future*—Today's rapidly changing and unpredictable world has rendered current educational offer less appropriate.
14. *Resource allocation*—In many countries the educational needs of young people are not always a priority, mainly due to economic and social reasons. Therefore, not enough resources are allocated to this important age group, neither by the countries nor by the do not community as a whole.
15. *Alliances and partnerships*—Effective alliances for quality education for young people are not sufficiently mobilized among students, teachers, parents, local communities, civil society, media, economic enterprises, the global community and other